Origins of CHINESE NAMES

Compiled by Asiapac Editorial
Illustrated by Fu Chunjiang
Translated by Choong Joo Ling and Chua Wei Lin

ASIAPAC • SINGAPORE

Publisher
ASIAPAC BOOKS PTE LTD
996 Bendemeer Road #06-09
Singapore 339944
Tel: (65) 6392 8455
Fax: (65) 6392 6455
Email: asiapacbooks@pacific.net.sg

Come visit us at our Internet home page
www.asiapacbooks.com

First published February 2007
2nd edition February 2008

© 2007 ASIAPAC BOOKS, SINGAPORE
ISBN 13 978-981-229-462-3
ISBN 10   981-229-462-7

All rights reserved. No part of this publication may be reproduced, stored in a retrieval system, or transmitted, in any form or by any means, electronic, mechanical, photocopying, recording, or otherwise, without the prior permission of the publisher. Under no circumstances shall it be rented, resold or redistributed. If this copy is defective, kindly exchange it at the above address.

Cover illustrations by Fu Chunjiang
Cover design by Chin Boon Leng
Body text in 11pt Times New Roman
Printed in Singapore by FuIsland Offset Printing (S) Pte Ltd

Publisher's Note

How Chinese names come about is a fascinating story that many people will be eager to learn. These names originate and develop in interesting and even bizarre ways. Family names originated from historical events and prevailing customs while given names are usually based on social considerations.

Many family names come from historical personalities although some come from the names of places and even unusual sources such as nature, numbers and even dynasties.

Most given names reflect parents' noble expectations but there are others that are whimsical in nature and anyone unfamiliar with Chinese culture and customs will find them bewildering. For example, names such as Little Dog or Waiting for Brother.

Besides captivating accounts, another invaluable feature of this book is a section on the 100 most common Chinese surnames which will give readers an insight into Chinese ancestry.

This book is the product of a collaborative effort on the part of the Asiapac editorial team to research and compile materials. We wish to thank Fu Chunjiang for his vibrant illustrations; Choong Joo Ling and Chua Wei Lin for the translation; and Koh Kok Kiang for his editorial support. Finally, we would like to show our appreciation to the production team for their hard work that has made this publication possible.

ORIGINS OF CHINESE MUSIC
Covers everything a music enthusiast wants to know about Chinese music: origins and history; Chinese musical instruments; classical masterpieces; and musicians of ancient China.
ISBN 978-981-229-475-3

CHINESE CULTURE SERIES
150x210mm, fully illustrated, 160-192 pages

 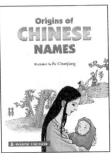  

978-981-229-475-3	Origins of Chinese Music
978-981-229-462-3	Origins of Chinese Names
078-981-229-242-1	Origins of Chinese People & Customs
978-981-229-378-7	Origins of Chinese Festivals
978-981-229-407-4	Origins of Chinese Culture
978-981-229-318-3	Origins of Chinese Food Culture
978-981-229-317-6	Origins of Chinese Cuisine
978-981-229-369-5	Origins of Chinese Tea & Wine
978-981-229-441-8	Origins of Chinese Art & Craft
978-981-229-376-3	Origins of Chinese Science & Technology
978-981-229-268-1	Origins of Chinese Martial Arts
978-981-229-408-1	Origins of Shaolin Kung Fu

About the Illustrator

Fu Chunjiang 傅春江 was born in Chongqing, China and received his BA in Chinese language and literature. A lover of Chinese culture, he is a versatile artist skilled in different styles, in particular the traditional style of comic books adapted from Chinese classics. His illustrations feature minute strokes, and clear and bright lines that can communicate the characters' rich and sincere feelings.

He has so far illustrated the following popular Asiapac titles: *Chinese Culture Pack*, *Origins of Chinese People and Customs*, *Origins of Chinese Culture*, *Gateway to Chinese Classical Literature*, *Essence of Traditional Chinese Medicine*, *Origins of Chinese Science and Technology*, *Origins of Chinese Festivals*, *Origins of Chinese Food Culture*, *Origins of Chinese Tea and Wine* and *Stories of Honour*.

Contents

Part One: Chinese Surnames — *1*

1. The genesis of surnames — *2*
2. How surnames were created — *12*
3. Bestowal and alteration of surnames — *16*
4. Classification of surnames — *28*
5. Major surnames — *35*
6. New hundred families' surnames — *37*

Part Two: Chinese Given Names — *101*

1. Origins of given names — *102*
2. Naming traditions — *103*
3. How names are chosen — *110*
4. Characteristics of naming throughout the ages — *120*
5. Names of commoners in ancient times — *121*
6. Emperor and names — *123*
7. Imperial examinations and names — *124*
8. Childhood names — *125*
9. Interesting names — *126*
10. Names and fortune — *128*
11. National and family name taboos — *131*
12. Customs of naming — *136*
13. Name repetition — *138*
14. Name riddles — *139*

Part Three: Courtesy Names and Other Types of Names — *141*

   1. Courtesy names — *142*
   2. Pseudonyms and nicknames — *145*
   3. Pen names and stage names — *149*

Part Four: The Chinese Way of Addressing — *151*

   1. Ways of calling Chinese names — *152*
   2. Self-referential and referential — *153*
   3. Forms of address from ancient to modern times — *156*
   4. Relationship Chart — *158*

Appendices

   Index of Chinese Family Names — *160*
   A Brief Chronology of Chinese History — *162*

Part One: Chinese Surnames

The variety of Chinese surnames is wide-ranging and colourful, with ancient origins, some going back as far as five or six thousand years. This section covers the genesis of surnames, the different ways they are formed, and the circumstances under which they may be changed, and origins of the 100 most common Chinese surnames.

1. The Genesis of Surnames

How Surnames Began

When people meet, they first exchange names. On finding someone with the same surname, they often feel a sense of kinship.

The Chinese people were the first to adopt surnames. Five to six thousand years ago, surnames were already in use. Where did surnames come from, then?

When did other countries begin using surnames?
Most European countries began using surnames around the Middle Ages; Korea, Vietnam and other Asian countries used surnames from around the 10th century. In Japan, the ordinary people were only allowed to have surnames in 1870.

The character for "xing姓(surname)" is formed from the characters "nü 女(woman)" and "sheng生(birth)". This reflects the matriarchal structure of ancient Chinese society which lasted until about 5,000 years ago. During that time, the mother was at the centre, forming a family unit with her children. There were few rules regarding marriage in these primitive societies, and people found that children born to closely related couples were more prone to birth defects and genetic abnormalities. Thus they began to distinguish blood ties using surnames. Children of the same mother shared a surname, and people with the same surname were not allowed to marry each other.

The ancient character form of "xing姓" was (human人 + birth生), implying human's creation and thus having surnames. The lateral radical "人" was later changed to "女": 姓 = 女 + 生

Character for surname found on bronzeware from the Spring and Autumn period (Human人 + Birth生)

Character for surname found carved on stone from the Warring States period (Birth生 + Woman女)

Character for surname found on texts from the Three Kingdoms period (Woman女 + Birth生)

Many ancient surnames carry the radical nü 女. The surnames of the ancestors of the Huaxia people and some benevolent kings in ancient times also had this radical.

Legendary Figures have no Fathers?

Besides Yandi and Huangdi, many other legendary figures have similar origins.

Huaxu 华胥 stepped onto a giant footprint left by the Thunder God and became pregnant, later giving birth to Fuxi 伏羲.

Nüjie 女节 gave birth to Shaohao 少昊 after sensing the presence of a shooting star.

Nüshu 女枢 gave birth to Zhuanxu 颛顼 after seeing a rainbow.

Qingdu 庆都 saw a crimson dragon and gave birth to Yao 尧.

Nüxi 女嬉 gave birth to Yu 禹 after swallowing the Job's tears plant.

Jiandi 简狄 gave birth to Qi 契 after swallowing a swallow's egg.

How clan names came about

After a prolonged period of time, people changed from a matriarchal society to a patriarchal society. As the number of descendants increased, a tribe was scattered into several branches living in different places. The descendants of each branch further identified themselves with names and this was how "Shi氏(clan name)" came about.

The ancient character form of "Shi".

The original meaning of Shi氏 was "plant's root". It was later explained as clan name, signifying the source of water and the basic of wood.

Shi氏(clan name) had its origins from Xing姓(surname). Many "Shi氏" could be derived from a "Xing姓". Descendants originating from the same Shi could be divided into groups having different Shi. E.g. Surname "Ji姬" was split into clan names of "Tang唐", "Jin晋" and "Yang杨".

During the Zhou Dynasty, Shi氏 was most numerously and commonly formed. With the implementation of the system of enfeoffment, lands were granted to princes under the emperor including his brothers, relatives and those of a different clan but who had rendered outstanding service. The descendants of these different states would then use their state name as their Shi.

When the feudal princes further bestowed some lands to their ministers, the latter's descendants would then adopt the name of the given city as their Shi. With the numerous instances of land division, many surnames which were based on the clan names from the given states and cities were thus formed.

Brother made Feudal Lord with a Tong Leaf

Shortly after the establishment of Zhou Dynasty, Zhou King Wu passed away and his young son Jisong ascended the throne and became King Cheng of Zhou, with the Duke of Zhou to assist him in the field of politics.

One day, while King Cheng was playing with his brother Shuyu叔虞, he picked up a tong leaf and trimmed it into the elongated shape of a pointed tablet of jade (held in the hands by ancient rulers on ceremonial occasions).

"This is for you. I'll make you a feudal lord."

The Duke of Zhou asked the king:

"You want to grant Shuyu a feudal state?"

"I'm only joking with my brother!"

"A sovereign must keep his promise!"

Hence King Cheng gave Tang state to Shuyu who became the state's feudal lord. Shuyu was later known as Tang Shuyu 唐叔虞. His descendants became his successors.

They moved to Jin晋 and changed their state title to Jin. During Duke Wu of Jin's reign, Yang state was granted to his second son Boqiao伯侨.

What is the difference between surname and clan name?

A surname (xing 姓) indicates the origin of one's blood lineage, whereas a clan name (shi 氏) branches out from a surname and further develops. Once a surname is formed, it is passed on from generation to generation. It will basically not be altered except in special situations. A clan name, however, might be changed when there were changes made to the conferred cities and official titles. Hence many different clan names may be derived from a single surname. There may also be people having similar clan names but different surnames.

The main purpose of having a surname is to identify different blood relationships. It is a basis of marriage. A clan name is used to distinguish one's status. During the Xia, Shang and Zhou dynasties, only people of the nobility had a clan name, while those of a humble family background had none.

The clear distinction between surname and clan name gradually became vague and they were combined during the Han Dynasty to be jointly called "xingshi 姓氏(surname)".

Legendary emperors Yandi and Huangdi: The founders of numerous Chinese surnames?

Tradition has it that in remote antiquity there were two famous tribes in the Yellow River Valley. One was Ji and had Huangdi (Yellow Emperor) as its chief. The other, Jiang, was headed by Yandi. Being closely related, they formed a tribal alliance. Huangdi lived by the Ji waterside, while Yandi stayed by the Jiang waterside, hence they used "Ji姬" and "Jiang姜" as their surnames respectively.

Yandi adopted "Jiang姜" as his surname, and over 200 surnames are derived from Yandi's surname including: Lü吕, Xu许, Cui崔, Ding丁, He贺, Lu卢, etc.

The population of Huangdi's descendants flourished. Among the five legendary emperors, Zhuanxu, Diku, Yao and Shun, and the Xia, Shang and Zhou dynasties' creators were said to have belonged to the lineage of Huangdi. Thus the number of surnames which have originated from Huangdi is greater than that of Yandi. Surnames that originated from Huangdi include: Zhang张, Wang王, Li李, Zhou周, Wu吴, etc.

2. How Surnames were Created

Worshipping totem as surname

A totem is an animal or natural object which the primitive men believed had a special relationship with their clan. It would also normally be used as the clan's symbol or name. A totem serves the same purpose as a "xing 姓 (surname)", that is, to distinguish one clan from another.

People of modern times will ask for each other's surname when they first meet, but when primitive tribesmen first met each other:

What is your totem?

Dragon.

As time went by, some totems were adopted as surnames, e.g. Long龙 (dragon), Feng凤 (phoenix), Xiong熊 (bear), Niao鸟 (bird), etc.

Horse.

Using the name of one's state
Examples include Qi 齐, Lu 鲁, Song 宋 and Wei 卫. These are names of states.

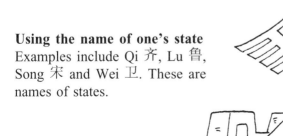

Using the name of one's fief
For example, during the Western Zhou Dynasty, there was a man by the name of Zaofu. He was rewarded with a fiefdom by Duke Mu of Zhou in Zhao city. Zaofu's descendants adopted the surname of Zhao.

Using the title of an official post
For example, Sima 司马 (Minister of War), Situ 司徒 (Minister of Land and People) and Sikong 司空 (Minister of Public Works) were titles of official posts in ancient times.

I'm the Minister of War (Sima 司马). My descendants shall take Sima as their surname.

I'm a potter. My surname is Tao 陶 (pottery) of course.

Using the name of one's occupation
For example, the ancestors of those whose surname is Tao were probably potters. Shamans and witchdoctors probably took on the surname Wu 巫.

Using the landmark of the place where one resided
Ximen 西门 (west gate), Liu 柳 (willow) and Chi 池 (pond) are just some examples. It is likely that these people lived near the west gate, some willow trees or a pond.

My surname is Liu 柳.

Ancestor's name as surname

During the Zhou Dynasty, the feudal state rulers' sons and grandsons were addressed as Gongzi 公子 and Gongsun 公孙 respectively. The great-grandsons and later generations would then use their great-grandfather's zi 字 (courtesy name) as their surname.

Some adopted their ancestors' name as the surname in order to commemorate them.

Son of Duke Mu of Deng   Grandson   Great-grandson

Seniority as surname

During ancient times, Bo 伯 or Meng 孟 indicated the eldest child, followed by Zhong 仲 (second), Shu 叔 (third) and Ji 季 (fourth). These characters were later used as surnames.

3. Bestowal and Alteration of Surnames

I, Wusong the overall head, will neither change my name nor surname!

In novels and dramas, when the heroes made their appearance and identified themselves, they would often conceitedly declare that they would neither change their name nor surname!

That's right! The Chinese have always valued their own surnames.

A surname is passed down from one's ancestors. Hence, the alteration of surname would be considered as an outrageous act of betrayal.

However, under certain compelled circumstances, situations of surname alteration do occur.

Emperor Yongle of the Ming Dynasty whose surname was Zhu conferred a special surname of Zheng on his eunuch, Ma He, who had served him with great loyalty for many years and who also helped him win a decisive battle which led to his becoming emperor. Ma He helped his 80,000-strong army rout a force of 500,000 led by general Li Jinglong who served the incumbent Emperor Jianwen.

Emperor Bestows Surname

In 1402, Zhu Di's army captured Nanjing and Emperor Jianwen was nowhere to be found. Zhu Di acceded to the throne and was known as Emperor Yongle in history.

The emperor would also confer his surname on his official who had rendered outstanding service. The emperor's surname was the most prestigious surname, also called "guoxing 国姓 (national surname)". The recipient of his surname was then known as "guoxingye 国姓爷". Those who shared the emperor's imperial surname were entitled to enjoy its privileges.

However, if one had annoyed the emperor, the latter would also give a bad surname to that person as a form of punishment, e.g. Xiao 枭 (fierce bird), Shao 蛸 (long-legged spider), Fu 蝮 (poisonous snake), etc.

During the reign of Liu Bang, founder of the Han Dynasty, who was known as Emperor Gaozu, Yingbu rose in rebellion but was captured.

When Yingbu was younger, he received a punishment called "qing 黥"(having words or marks carved on a criminal's face and painting them black).

You and your descendants will all bear the surname of "Qing 黥"!

During the Qing Dynasty, there was a Ma family in Shandong which had once offended Emperor Yongzheng. He changed their surname so that the family members would be scolded by others and their descendants would be of humble status.

Change of Surname

For most people who had changed their surnames, they did it in order to avoid any misfortune, enmity or taboo.

Duke Wu of Zheng during the Spring and Autumn period was succeeded by his elder son, who was known as Duke Zhuang. Shuduan was his second son. Under the instigation of his mother, Shuduan launched a coup.

When the plot failed, Shuduan fled to Gong 共 (today's Hui county, Henan) and named himself Gong Shuduan.

His descendants adopted "Gong 共" as their surname. The Gong families later added the character "Long 龙" to their surname character in order to forestall any disaster. Hence, their surname then became "Gong 龚".

In the past, if one's surname was identical or similar to the emperors' or sages' names, then the usage of that surname would be avoided as a taboo. For instance, Han Dynasty Emperor Wudi was named Liu Che, so those having Che 彻 as their surname would then change it to "Tong 通"; Emperor Xuandi was called Liu Xun 刘荀, thus people whose surname was Xun 荀 would change it to Sun 孙 instead.

Carps Forbidden because of Emperor's Surname Li?

The Surname that was Altered Repeatedly

A Surname that became Six Surnames?

In the Putian district of Fujian province, there exists the famous "Liu Gui Tang 六桂堂 (Hall of Six Laurels)". It is a common ancestral hall shared by people with these six surnames: Weng 翁, Hong 洪, Jiang 江, Fang 方, Gong 龔 and Wang 汪. Why are they using the same ancestral hall? This is because these surnames have all been derived from the single surname Weng 翁. During the Five Dynasties period, somebody by the name of Weng Qiandu 翁乾度 served as a physician to King Min of the Min kingdom which was later destroyed by the Southern Tang kingdom. In order to avoid any disaster, Weng Qiandu gave each of his six sons a different surname. All the six sons were successful candidates of the government examination, so they were called the Six Victory Laurels and their later generations named the ancestral hall as "Six Laurels".

Previously, a family which had only daughters would invite their son-in-law to marry into the family so as to have a male heir. The son-in-law and offspring would adopt the bride's surname. But there were some who would rather give up beauty and wealth than to abandon their own surname.

Beauty Forsaken, Surname Retained

Tang Dynasty poet Rong Yu won the admiration of Assistant Minister Cui. But...

I don't like your surname. If you can change it, I'll allow you to marry my daughter.

As Miss Cui was a well-known beauty, Rong Yu hesitated...

Do I want beauty or surname? A beauty is hard to come by, a surname can easily be altered...

After much consideration, Rong Yu finally turned down the marriage. He would rather retain his surname than have a rare beauty.

Adoption of Chinese surnames by the national minorities

The largest scale of Chinese surname adoption that had ever taken place occurred during the Northern and Southern Dynasties period. Northern Wei Dynasty Emperor Xiaowen of the Xianbei 鲜卑 nationality ordered the surnames of the Xianbei people to be changed to Chinese surnames, and a total of 144 surnames were altered.

In China, many national minorities from distant lands used to enter and settle down in the Central Plains occupied by the Chinese people. They would even build up their political power and dynasties. For example, the Yuan and Qing Dynasties were established by the Mongolians and Manchurians respectively. Hence, most people of the national minorities would adopt a Chinese surname.

Xianbei surname	Chinese surname (after localisation)
Tuoba 拓跋 (a royal surname)	Yuan 元
Helu 贺鲁	Zhou 周
Qujin 去斤	Ai 艾
Chiluo 叱罗	Luo 罗
Keba 柯拔	Ke 柯
Qiumu 丘穆	Mu 穆
Buliugu 步六孤	Lu 陆

Manchurian surname	Chinese surname (after localisation)
Suochuoluo 索绰罗	Suo 索
Wanyan 完颜	Wang 汪 / 王
Guaerjia 瓜尔佳	Guan 关
Yiergenjueluo 伊尔根觉罗	Zhao 赵
Niuhulu 纽祜禄	Lang 郎
Qijiashi 齐佳氏	Qi 齐

Sometimes, the Chinese emperors would also confer Chinese surnames on the national minorities' chiefs or those who had contributed great services. Han Dynasty Emperor Wudi once gave Midi, the crown prince of Xiongnu King Xiutu, the surname of "Jin 金". This Xiongnu person thus became a holder of the surname Jin 金. He later settled in the capital Chang'an (today's Xi'an) and his seven generations of descendants became influential officials.

Self-created Surnames

Blood-kin Sisters having Different Surnames

Some couples fought over "surname rights" and compromised to have a compound surname.

Some fathers will also use their names to form their children's surname. For example, for a father whose surname is Shu 舒 and name is Ke 克, his daughter's compound surname will be "Shuke 舒克".

The all-in-one Ancestral Surname "Dian点"!

There was a newborn baby whose paternal grandfather's and grandmother's surnames were Jiang蒋 and Song宋 and his maternal grandfather's and grandmother's surnames were Bian卞 and Shen沈.

According to tradition, this child will follow his father's surname Jiang蒋.

Times have changed. We should let him follow his mother's surname Bian卞.

Paternal grandpa

Maternal grandpa

No! No! He'll be called Little Bian/Xiaobian 小便(urine) and later Big Bian/Dabian 大便 (faeces). Use surname Shen沈!

Maternal grandma

Paternal grandma

Hey! Even if he should adopt a surname from the female side, he should use my surname Song宋.

The child will adopt surname "Dian点"!

Why is "Dian点" chosen?

Father

Look, the four dots at the bottom of the character "Dian点" represent the four surnames of our forefathers.

The upper character component "Zhan占(occupy)" indicates that the child belongs to his ancestors of all the four surnames.

Hence the surname of this child becomes "Dian点".

> The alteration of surnames may be an indication of openness and democracy. But a surname is more than just a symbol, it carries significant meaning of blood relationship. One should be cautious about the changing of surnames because this may lead to confusion in blood relationship.

Foreign Surnames

Through the interaction of Chinese with foreigners in the past, some surnames were formed consequently. For example, the surname "An安" came from Anxi 安息 (a country in what is now north-eastern Iran). It is recorded that that the prince of Anxi country came to China to propagate religion. He used his country name "An 安" as his surname, and his name was Qing. He settled in China and his later generations adopted his surname "An 安". Most of them lived around the north-western regions.

During the Ming Dynasty, the King of Sulu State 苏禄国 (today's Philippines) Baduge Bahala 巴都葛. 巴哈剌 visited China. The king later passed away in Dezhou city of Shandong province, and Emperor Yongle held a grand funeral for him. King Baduge's sons Wenhala 温哈剌, Andulu 安都鲁 and their wives remained in China. The descendants of Wenhala and Andulu were then born and bred in China, having "Wen温" and "An安" as their surnames.

4. Classification of Surnames

According to the *Grand Dictionary of Chinese Surnames,* there exist 11,939 Chinese surnames in total throughout history!

But quite a number of surnames have already became obsolete. There are only over 3,000 Chinese surnames currently in use, and only about 500 of them are commonly used.

The well-known book "Baijiaxing 百家姓 (The Hundred Families' Surnames)" contains a hundred most commonly seen surnames, compiled by a scholar in Qiantang (Hangzhou) during the Northern Song Dynasty. The order of surnames are not arranged according to the size of population bearing the surname. Four surnames are arranged in a row such that the pronunciation runs smooth and rhythmic, making learning and remembering easy. Initially, the book had compiled 411 surnames. More were added later and the total number of surnames became 504. Among them, 444 surnames were single characters and 60 of them were compound surnames.

Why were Zhao Qian Sun Li, Zhou Wu Zheng Wang arranged at the beginning of the book?

Baijiaxing was compiled by an unknown Song Dynasty scholar who lived in the boundary area between the Wu 吴 and Yue 越 regions (today's Hangzhou city, Zhejiang province). "Zhao Qian Sun Li 赵钱孙李" was arranged at the beginning of the book because the Song Dynasty emperor's surname was Zhao 赵; During the Five Dynasties period, the surname of the Wuyue kingdom rulers was Qian 钱; "Sun 孙" was the surname of Wuyue King Qianshu's concubine; "Li 李" was the surname of the Southern Tang Dynasty ruler.

As for the second row of surnames "Zhou Wu Zheng Wang 周吴郑王", they were the surnames of Song Dynasty emperors' concubines.

Compound Surnames

Most Chinese surnames are single characters, and only a few are compound surnames. Many compound surnames have been broken down to become a single-character surname.

Development of compound surnames to single-character surnames

From a compound surname to two single-character surnames:

Ouyang 欧阳　- Ou 欧, Yang 阳
Sima 司马　- Si 司, Ma 马
Zhuge 诸葛　- Zhu 诸, Ge 葛
Mengsun 孟孙　- Meng 孟, Sun 孙

Omission of a word in a compound surname to form a single-character surname:

Dongguo 东郭　- Guo 郭
Situ 司徒　- Si 司
Zuoren 左人　- Zuo 左
Gongxia 公夏　- Xia 夏

Some compound surnames have existed for a long time, e.g. Sikong司空, Situ司徒, Sima司马 were official titles used in the past.

Situ司徒: an official who was in charge of managing the country's land, people and education. Shun舜 had once been a Situ of Yao尧, thus some of Shun's descendants adopted "Situ" as their surname.

Sikong司空: a title created by the person in charge, ancient hero Great Yu大禹 was a "Sikong" of Yao before, so his descendants later used "Sikong" as their surname.

Sima司马: an official who took charge of military affairs. During Zhou King Xuan's reign, Chengbo Xiufu 程伯休父 held the official position of Sima. His descendants' surname were therefore "Sima". Western Han Dynasty historian Sima Qian 司马迁 once claimed that he was the offspring of Xiufu. Some compound surnames originated from the national minorities, e.g. Murong慕容, Zhangsun 长孙 and Yuchi 尉迟 are surnames of the Xianbei 鲜卑 nationality.

Most compound surnames are made up of two characters, some had three, four, five or even up to nine characters. Those which consist of more than three characters are usually surnames of the national minorities, e.g. Salige 撒里哥, Dadazhang 答答丈, Yan-bu-hua-dai 颜不华歹, A-da-li-ji-dai 阿大里吉歹, Wa-zhi-la-sun-da-li 瓦只剌孙答里, etc.

Interesting compound surname Yangshe 羊舌

During the Spring and Autumn period, there were people with the surname "Yangshe 羊舌" in the state of Jin 晋. They include "Yangshe Zhi 羊舌职", "Yangshe Hu 羊舌虎", "Yangshe Chi 羊舌赤".

The original surname of Mr Yangshe was Ji 季 and his name was Guo 果. One day, somebody stole a sheep and gave the sheep's head to Ji Guo.

Don't stand on ceremony, just take it! It doesn't cost me a cent anyway.

This is stolen stuff, I mustn't eat it. I shall bury it!

The thief later implicated Ji Guo in the theft.

Ji Guo had eaten the sheep's head, so he was involved!

Ji Guo dug out the sheep's head in order to prove his innocence.

I didn't eat the sheep's head!

By then, the sheep's head had already turned rotten. Only the sheep's tongue remained. Hence Ji Guo was spared punishment.

To mark this incident, Ji Guo adopted "Yangshe 羊舌 (sheep's tongue)" as his surname.

Interesting surnames

Surnames based on:
Colours
Huang黄 (yellow), Hong红 (red), Zhu朱 (vermilion), Bai白 (white), Mo墨 (black), Lan蓝 (blue), Qing青 (green), Hui灰 (grey), Zi紫 (purple or violet)
Positions
Dong东 (east), Nan南 (south), Xi西 (west), Bei北 (north), Shang上 (above), Xia下 (below), Zuo左 (left), You右 (right), Qian前 (front), Hou后 (back)
Seasons
Chun春 (spring), Xia夏 (summer), Qiu秋 (autumn), Dong冬 (winter)
Dynasties
Xia夏, Shang商, Zhou周, Qin秦, Han汉, Jin晋, Wei魏, Shu蜀, Wu吴 Sui隋, Tang唐, Song宋, Yuan元, Ming明, Qing清
Plants
Hua花 (flower), Mei梅 (plum), Ye叶 (leaf), Yang杨 (poplar), Liu柳 (willow), Song松 (pine), Gui桂 (cassia), Miao苗 (sprout), Lin林 (forest), Tao桃 (peach)
Insects
Chong虫 (worm), Chan蝉 (cicada), Can蚕 (silkworm), E蛾 (moth), Yi蚁 (ant)
Nature
Shan山 (mountain), Gu谷 (valley), Shui水 (water), Yun云 (cloud), Jiang江 (river), Lei雷 (thunder), Chi池 (pond), Sha沙 (sand), Hong虹 (rainbow), Xing星 (star)
Numbers
Ling零 (zero), Yi一 (one), Er二 (two), San三 (three), Si四 (four), Wu五 (five), Liu六 (six), Qi七 (seven), Ba八 (eight), Jiu九 (nine), Shi十 (ten) Bai百 (hundred), Qian千 (thousand), Wan万 (ten thousand)

Surnames can be classified in many interesting ways.

Yes! There are surnames based on dynasties, colours and numbers.

There are surnames of "death" and "disaster"?

There exists a rare surname of "Si死(death)" mainly around the northwestern region of China. It originated from a national minority's compound surname during the Northern Wei Dynasty.

Those who bear the surname "Nan难(disaster)" are found mainly in Henan province. This surname came about from the Xianbei national minority during the Northern and Southern Dynasties period. It was said that "Nan" originally referred to a type of bird. The ancient people were fond of birds, so "Nan" was adopted as their surname. These Xianbei people having the surname Nan later travelled northwards. Most of them resided in North Korea and few were left in China.

Some even have Gao糕(cake), Jiu酒(wine) and Cha茶(tea) as surnames!

These interesting surnames are very rare!

Who is "Bigger"? – Numeral Surnames

Many Chinese characters share the same pronunciation. Hence, take care not to mispronounce characters.

Some commonly mispronounced surnames:
Qiu仇, not "chou" as in "**chouhen**仇恨".
Ou区, not "qu" as in "**diqu**地区".
Ren任, not "ren" as in "**renwu**任务".
Piao朴, not "pu" as in "**pusu**朴素".
Shan单, not "dan" as in "**gudan**孤单".
Ji纪, not "ji" as in "**jinian**纪念".
Zha查, not "cha" as in "**jiancha**检查".
Xian洗, not "xi" as in "**xidi**洗涤".
Xie解, not "jie" as in "**jiefang**解放".
Yun员, not "yuan" as in "**chengyuan**成员".

How should 乐乐乐 be pronounced?

5. Major Surnames

There's a popular folk saying that the surnames of Zhang张, Wang王, Li李, Zhao赵 and Liu刘 are very widespread.

Zhang张, Wang王, Li李, Zhao赵 and Liu刘 are very common Chinese surnames with a large number of people having these surnames. They are some examples of "major surnames".

Most ancient or modern major surnames are of long standing and used extensively. For example, there are at least ten origins of the surname Wang王. Some of these surnames came from national surnames such as Li李, Liu刘 and Zhao赵 which are surnames of the Tang, Han and Song Dynasties' emperors respectively. In ancient times, people with national surnames could enjoy special privileges. During the Han Dynasty, those who had the surname "Liu刘" were exempted from paying taxes and getting enlisted in the army. The emperors would also confer the national surname on subjects who had rendered great service. Moreover, the emperors had numerous concubines who would produce many offspring bearing the surname Liu刘. Hence there was an increase of population having the surname Liu刘.

Major surnames of the rich

In every dynasty, there would be major surnames from eminent families. During the Wei and Jin Dynasties period, Wang王 and Sima司马 were said to be the dominating surnames of that era, that is to say, the Wang noble families and the Sima emperors had great dominating power over the people. As for the Tang Dynasty, major surnames of the rich such as Cui崔, Lu卢, Li李 and Zheng郑 were predominant. A total of 27 prime ministers had the surname "Cui崔" during the Tang Dynasty. The people having these major surnames held on to the concept of family status very strongly. Hence, they would prefer that their daughters remain single than to have them married to the common people.

Not only was the betrothal to an ordinary commoner disallowed, if they did not like an emperor's origin, they would also not agree to the marriage!

As there had been cross marriages between the Tang Dynasty imperial families and the national minorities, many notable families of major surnames were unwilling to arrange marriages with the imperial members.

6. New Hundred Families' Surnames

According to the investigation and research carried out by the China Institute of Genetics and Developmental Biology in 2006, a new set of the 100 most common families' surnames in China is listed in descending order:

Li李, Wang王, Zhang张, Liu刘, Chen陈, Yang杨, Huang黄, Zhao赵, Zhou周, Wu吴, Xu徐, Sun孙, Zhu朱, Ma马, Hu胡, Guo郭, Lin林, He何, Gao高, Liang梁, Zheng郑, Luo罗, Song宋, Xie谢, Tang唐, Han韩, Cao曹, Xu许, Deng邓, Xiao萧, Feng冯, Zeng曾, Cheng程, Cai蔡, Peng彭, Pan潘, Yuan袁, Yu于, Dong董, Yu余, Su苏, Ye叶, Lü吕, Wei魏, Jiang蒋, Tian田, Du杜, Ding丁, Shen沈, Jiang姜, Fan范, Jiang江, Fu傅, Zhong钟, Lu卢, Wang汪, Dai戴, Cui崔, Ren任, Lu陆, Liao廖, Yao姚, Fang方, Jin金, Qiu邱, Xia夏, Tan谭, Wei韦, Jia贾, Zou邹, Shi石, Xiong熊, Meng孟, Qin秦, Yan阎, Xue薛, Hou侯, Lei雷, Bai白, Long龙, Duan段, Hao郝, Kong孔, Shao邵, Shi史, Mao毛, Chang常, Wan万, Gu顾, Lai赖, Wu武, Kang康, He贺, Yan严, Yin尹, Qian钱, Shi施, Niu牛, Hong洪, Gong龚

Surnames of Overseas Chinese

As the saying goes, "all surnames are of a same root". Most Chinese surnames originated from the Central Plains, but usually many surname branches have gone through the coastal regions such as Fujian and Guangdong provinces and moved outwards, taking root abroad and expanding in size. In Taiwan, the Chen陈 and Lin林 surnames are very widespread, and the surnames of Huang黄 and Zheng郑 are also quite common. Other commonly known Chinese surnames in Taiwan include: Zhang张, Li李, Wang王, Wu吴, Cai蔡, Liu刘, Yang杨, Xu许, Xie谢, Guo郭, Lai赖, Zeng曾, Hong洪, Qiu邱, Zhou周, Ye叶, Liao廖, Xu徐, Zhuang庄, Su苏, Jiang江 and He何. There are about 300 Chinese surnames used in Singapore, of which the commonly known ones are Chen陈, Lin林, Huang黄, Li李, Wang王, Zhang张, Wu吴, Cai蔡, Liu刘 and Yang杨.

Origins of the Surname Li 李

The origins of Li can be traced to the late Shang Dynasty and early Zhou Dynasty. Its original form was 理 (Li) and was first used by Gaoyao. He served King Yao as a senior justice official. The position was named Dali 大理. His descendants inherited his post.

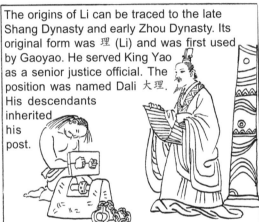

By the Shang Dynasty, it was the norm for the names of official positions to be used as the surname. Thus his descendants adopted the surname Li 理.

King Zhou of the late Shang Dynasty was a tyrant. One of Gaoyao's descendants, Li Zheng 理徵, boldly pointed out his mistakes, and urged him to mend his ways. King Zhou was furious and killed him. Li Zheng's wife fled with her young son Li Lizhen 理利真 to the west of Henan.

Mother and son arrived at the ruins of the Yi tribe settlement at the Yi River basin. They were hungry and thirsty.

Mother, can we eat this wild fruit?

Sure, *muzi* can quench your thirst and sate your hunger.

They lived on *muzi* and survived. Grateful for the wild fruit, and also to avoid King Zhou's persecution, Li Lizhen combined the two characters of *muzi* 木子 to create the character *li* 李. He used that as his surname.
This is how surname Li came about.

Famous Li figures:

Li was the surname of the emperors of the Tang Dynasty

Li Er 李耳 was the name of Laozi, the great philosopher who lived during the Spring and Autumn period

Li Bai 李白 was the name of the famous Tang poet

Origins of the Surname Wang 王

The Wangs' ancestors were all descendants of the royal families from the Shang and Zhou Dynasties. Hence people would call them "wangjia王家 (royal family)". Their later generations then used "Wang王" as their surname.

King Ling of Zhou had a bright crown prince named Jin晋. Jin once had some disagreement with King Ling on the issue of river regulating, and was stripped of his title.

"Since you go against me, I shall strip you of your title."

Jin went to live in Langya琅琊 in Shandong. As he was a descendant of Zhou kings, the locals thus called him wangjia王家. There were other nationalities...

...that bore the surname Wang. Wang Kon王建 was the founder of Korea's Koryo Dynasty (918-1392) and Wang Xiong王雄 was the ancestor of those surnamed Kepin可频 during the Western Jin Dynasty.

Famous Wang figures:
One of the "Four Beauties of China" Wang Zhaojun王昭君, the great Eastern Jin calligrapher Wang Xizhi王羲之, Northern Song premier Wang Anshi王安石, Tang poets Wang Wei王维, Wang Changling王昌龄, Wang Zhihuan王之涣, Wang Bo王勃, Northern Song medical scientist Wang Weiyi王惟一 and the Yuan author of *Romance of the Western Chamber*, Wang Shifu王实甫.

Origins of the Surname Zhang 张

Huangdi's descendant Hui was said to have invented the bow.

Bow and arrow are the most vital weapons. I'll make you Supervisor of Bow and Arrow Makers.

Your surname shall be Zhang 张.

The old script of Zhang resembles that of a man drawing his bow. That is how the surname Zhang came about.

Famous Zhang figures:

Zhang Qian 张骞, the diplomat who opened the Silk Road

Zhang Heng 张衡, a scientist during the Eastern Han Dynasty

Origins of the Surname Liu 刘

King Yao's surname was said to be Yiqi 伊祁. A branch of his descendants adopted Qi 祁 as their surname. They were given land in Liuguo 刘国.

Liu Lei 刘累, a descendant of the Qi branch, supposedly acquired the knowledge of rearing dragons from Huanlong.

Liu Lei failed to keep the dragons alive and fled with his family to Lu county. All his descendants bore the surname Liu 刘.

Famous Liu figures:

Liu was the surname of Han Dynasty emperors.

Liu Bowen 刘伯温 was a famous military tactician of the Ming Dynasty.

Origins of the Surname Chen 陈

After King Wu of Zhou toppled the Shang Dynasty, he conferred titles and land on the descendants of good officials. On finding King Shun's descendant Gui Man 妫满, King Wu married his eldest daughter, Yuanji, to him and gave him the title "Marquis Chen".

Yao married his two daughters to Shun and let them settle down by Guirui River. Their descendants who remained by there used the surname Gui 妫.

His descendants adopted the surname Chen 陈.

Famous Chen figures:

Tang poet Chen Zi'ang 陈子昂

Chinese patriot in modern times, Chen Jiageng 陈嘉庚 (Tan Kah Kee)

Origins of the Surname Yang 杨

Origins of the Surname Huang 黄

Boyi伯益 had rendered a great service to Great Yu大禹 by regulating rivers, hence Emperor Shun conferred the surname of "Ying 嬴" on him.

Boyi gave some land to some who shared his surname. Among them, some were given the Huang region (today's western Huangchuan, Henan). They established the state of Huang, with descendants having surname "Huang黄".

Famous Huang figures:
Dutiful son Huang Xiang黄香 during the Eastern Han Dynasty

Northern Song Dynasty poet Huang Tingjian黄庭坚

Yuan Dynasty female weaver Huang Daopo黄道婆

Ming Dynasty Neo-Confucian philosopher Huang Zongxi黄宗羲

Origins of the Surname Zhao 赵

Zaofu was a carriage driver serving King Mu of the Zhou Dynasty.

One day, King Mu headed west and went hunting in a carriage drawn by swift steeds. Upon arriving at Mt Kunlun, he drank and sang with the Queen Mother of the West and forgot to return.

At this time, Duke Xuyan in the southeast rebelled. Zaofu's driving skills were fully displayed as he travelled thousands of *li* in just a day. They returned in time.

Origins of the Surname Zhou 周

The earliest ancestor of the Zhou people was Houji后稷. Houji's mother stepped onto the toe print of Sky King and became pregnant. After his birth, Houji was abandoned in the wild.

An eagle wrapped baby Houji with its wings to keep him warm. Cows and goats would also feed Houji with their milk.

Houji grew up and knew how to grow a hundred types of grain.

Houji's descendants lived in Tai邰 (today's western Wugong county, Shaanxi) at first, later residing at Zhouyuan周原 (today's Weihe plain in Shaanxi). Hence they were also known as the Zhou clan, but their surname was, however, Ji姬. It was after the collapse of the Zhou Dynasty that the later generations then adopted the surname "Zhou".

Famous Zhou figures:
Three Kingdoms period well-known general Zhou Yu周瑜, Song Dynasty poet Zhou Bangyan周邦彦, Song Dynasty philosopher Zhou Dunyi周敦颐, Modern China eminent writers Zhou Shuren周树人and Zhou Zuoren周作人, China's ex-prime minister Zhou Enlai周恩来.

Origins of the Surname Wu 吴

Zhou King Tai周太王, the Zhou clan's earliest ancestor, had two elder sons Taibo太伯 and Zhongyong仲雍 who left the Zhou clan in order to let their younger brother Jili季历 ascend the throne. They went on to Suzhou and established the state of Wu instead.

During the late Spring and Autumn period, Wu state was destroyed by Yue state. But some descendants of Wu would still use the state's name as their surname.

Famous Wu figures: Warring States period military strategist Wu Qi 吴起

Wu Guang吴广, who started a peasant uprising during the Qin Dynasty

Tang Dynasty artist Wu Daozi吴道子

Origins of the Surname Xu 徐

Yu, the founder of the Xia Dynasty, bestowed the feudal state of Xu徐 (today's north-western Jiangsu and north-eastern Anhui regions) on Boyi's son Ruomu若木. During the Western Zhou Dynasty, a descendant of Ruomu named Xuyan徐偃 dug out a pair of red bow and arrow.

He thought this was predestined, hence he rose in rebellion against the Zhou ruler. Zhou King Mu rushed back to the capital from Mount Kunlun, and defeated Duke Xuyan.

But knowing that Xuyan was popular among the local people, King Mu made him the ruler of Xu state. Xu was later destroyed by Wu state, but the descendants of Xu state still used their state's name as their surname.

Famous Xu figures: Ming Dynasty scientist Xu Guangqi徐光启, Ming Dynasty geographer Xu Xiake徐霞客, Modern China artist Xu Beihong徐悲鸿 and poet Xu Zhimo徐志摩.

Origins of the Surname Sun 孙

There are three origins of "Sun孙": One was from the surname Ji姬. Zhou King Wen's son Kangshu康叔 was made the ruler of Wei卫 state. His eighth generation grandson Wu helped to defeat troops in the west and hence was conferred the title of Duke.

Duke Wu of Wei's great-grandson Wuzhong was also known as Sunzhong孙仲. The later generations then adopted "Sun" as their surname.

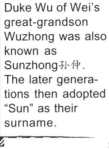

The surname "Sun" also came from the descendants of the Chu state magistrate Sun Shuao孙叔敖.

The third origin came from senior official Tianshu田书 of Qi state. He had made contributions to the country, and was thus rewarded with the surname "Sun".

Famous Sun figures:

Spring and Autumn period military strategist Sunzi孙子

Tang Dynasty medical scientist Sun Simiao孙思邈

"Father of Modern China" Sun Yat-sen孙中山

Origins of the Surname Zhu 朱

The surname "Zhu" originated from three sources:
One of them originated from Caoxie 曹挟, a descendant of legendary emperor Zhuanxu 颛顼. During Zhou King Wu's reign, Caoxie was given the state of Zhu 邾 (today's Zou 邹 county, Shandong). Zhu state was later destroyed by Chu state, and the descendants took "Zhu 朱" as their surname.

The second origin came from the descendants of Zhuhu 朱虎 whose surname was Zhu 朱. Zhuhu was an official of legendary emperor Shun.

The third origin came about during the Northern Wei Dynasty when emperor Xiao Wendi changed the Xianbei tribe's surnames to Chinese surnames, e.g. surnames Zhuohun 浊浑 and Kezhuhun 可朱浑 were changed to "Zhu 朱".

Famous Zhu figures:

Zhu Yuanzhang 朱元璋, founder of the Ming Dynasty

Zhu Shuzhen 朱淑贞, Song Dynasty female poet

Zhu Xi 朱熹, Neo-Confucian philosopher of the Southern Song Dynasty

Origins of the Surname Ma 马

The ancestor of Ma descendants was general Zhao She赵奢 of the Warring States period. He was given the state of Mafu马服(today's north-western Handan, Hebei).

"Mr Mafu" thus became a pseudonym for him, and his descendants had the surname "Ma马".

Famous Ma figures:

Eastern Han Dynasty great general Ma Yuan马援

Three Kingdoms period mechanism maker Ma Jun马钧

Yuan Dynasty dramatist Ma Zhiyuan马致远

Origins of the Surname Hu 胡

The surname "Hu" had three origins.
During the Western Zhou Dynasty, a feudal state was given to a descendant of Yushun 虞舜.

After his death, a laudatory posthumous name "Chen Hugong 陈胡公" was bestowed on him. Thus his later generations had their surname as "Hu 胡".

The other two origins of "Hu" came about from two Hu states during the Zhou Dynasty. Their descendants later used the state name as their surname.

Famous Hu figures:

Empress Dowager Hu of Northern Wei Dynasty

Ming Dynasty general Hu Dahai 胡大海

Modern China scholar Hu Shi 胡适

Origins of the Surname Guo 郭

The ancestor of the Guo people was Zhou King Wen's brother Guo Shu虢叔. Guo Shu was a feudal lord of the state of Guo虢.

Jin state later wiped out Guo state.

The state name "Guo虢" became the later generations' surname.

As Guo虢 and Guo郭 are very similar in pronunciation, some people switched to using the latter surname.

Famous Guo figures:

Western Han Dynasty pugilist Guo Xie郭解

Yuan Dynasty scientist Guo Shoujing郭守敬

Modern China writer Guo Moruo郭沫若

Origins of the Surname Lin 林

King Zhou, the last king of the Shang Dynasty, took pleasure in torturing and killing the innocent.

Loyal official Bigan 比干 remonstrated with the king and was put to death.

Bigan's wife, who was pregnant, escaped to the forest and later gave birth to a son.

After King Wu of Zhou destroyed the Shang regime,...

...he bestowed the name Lin 林 on Bigan's son, and also made him his official.

Famous personalities with the surname Lin:

Modern writer Lin Yutang 林语堂

Lin Zexu 林则徐, the Qing official who tried to stamp out opium

Origins of the Surname He 何

The surname "He" actually originated from the surname "Han韩". A descendant of Tang Shuyu 唐叔虞 was given the state of Han. His descendants' surname was then "Han韩". After Han state was eliminated by Qin state, the later generations dispersed.

Some of them fled to the Huaijiang 淮江 region.

Han韩" and "He何" sounded similarly locally. In order to avoid Qin's pursuers, the escapees changed their surname to "He何".

"Sir, you don't look like a local. Your surname?"

"My surname is...He何."

Famous He figures:

Han Dynasty great general He Jin 何进

Modern China poet He Qifang 何其芳

Origins of the Surname Gao 高

During the Western Zhou Dynasty, the state of Gao 高 (today's Yu 禹 county, Henan) was given to Duke Wen of Qi's son. Hence he was addressed as "Gongzi Gao 公子高 (Young Master Gao)." His grandchild was Xi.

Xi worked with the minister of Qi state to kill rebel Gongsun Wuzhi.

He welcomed Young Master Xiaobai (Duke Huan of Qi 齐桓公, one of the "Five Hegemons" during the Spring and Autumn period), as the state ruler.

Duke Huan then granted Xi's grandfather's name "Gao 高" as Xi's surname.

Famous Gao figures:

Warring States period swordsman Gao Jianli 高渐离

Tang Dynasty poet Gao Shi 高适

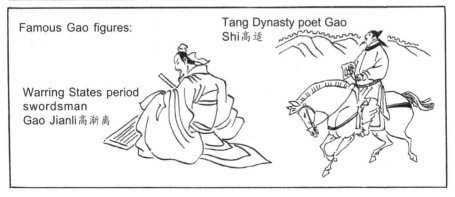

Origins of the Surname Liang 梁

The Liang's ancestry can be traced back to Boyi 伯益 of the Xia Dynasty.

During Zhou King Xuan's reign, Qinzhong 秦仲, one of Boyi's descendants, was killed when he went on a punitive expedition against the western troops.

Qinzhong's five sons avenged his death and defeated the enemy.

King Xuan rewarded them with feudal states. The second son was made the lord of Liangshan (today's Han 韩 city, Shaanxi). The state name "Liang 梁" became the surname of his descendants.

Famous Liang figures:

Southern Song Dynasty female general Liang Hongyu 梁红玉

Modern China scholar and reformist Liang Qichao 梁启超

Origins of the Surname Zheng 郑

King Xuan of Zhou gave state of Zheng郑 (today's eastern Hua华 county, Shaanxi) to his brother Jiyou姬友 who was also addressed as Duke Huan of Zheng 郑桓公.

During Zhou King You's reign, the Western Zhou Dynasty was falling, so Duke Huan went to seek advice from an imperial historian.

At the central region of Henan where the He河, Luo洛, Ji济 and Ying颍 rivers flow, the locations are good.

Hence he went to live there and his son Duke Wu郑武公 later built the Zheng郑 state around the Xinzheng area. Zheng state was ultimately destroyed by Han state, but his descendants bore the state name "Zheng".

Famous Zheng figures: Ming Dynasty great naval navigator Zheng He郑和, Ming Dynasty military leader Zheng Chenggong郑成功 who recovered Taiwan, Qing Dynasty writer, calligrapher cum artist Zheng Banqiao郑板桥.

Origins of the surname Luo 罗

There were two states of Luo (today's western Yi 宜 city, Hubei) during the Zhou Dynasty. They were eliminated by Chu state during the Spring and Autumn period, and their descendants used the state name "Luo 罗" as their surname.

Those having the surnames of Poduoluo 破多罗, Chiluo 叱罗 (during Northern Wei Dynasty), Huseluo 斛瑟罗 (during Tang Dynasty) and Aixinjueluo 爱新觉罗 (during Qing Dynasty) had all changed them to the surname "Luo 罗".

Famous Luo figures:
Sui and Tang Dynasties well-known general Luo Cheng 罗成

Yuan Dynasty to early Ming Dynasty novelist Luo Guanzhong 罗贯中

Origins of the Surname Song 宋

The ancestor of the Song people was Shang Dynasty King Zhou's brother Wei Ziqi 微子启.

After King Wu of Zhou overthrew the Shang Dynasty, Wei Ziqi was conferred the title of Songgong 宋公 (Duke of Song), thus the latter's descendants were of the surname "Song 宋" also.

Famous Song figures:

Warring States period writer Song Yu 宋玉

Tang Dynasty poet Song Zhiwen 宋之问

The well-known "Three Soong Sisters" of Modern China: Song Qingling 宋庆龄, Song Ailing 宋霭龄, Song Meiling 宋美龄.

Origins of the Surname Xie 谢

During the Western Zhou Dynasty, Zhou King Xuan granted the state of Xie谢 (today's Tanghe唐河 county, Henan) to his mother's brother Shenhou申侯.

Xie state was later lost to the Chu and Qin states. Its descendants had "Xie谢" as their surname.

Famous Xie figures:

Eastern Jin Dynasty prime minister Xie An 谢安

Southern Dynasties poet Xie Lingyun谢灵运

Origins of the Surname Tang 唐

Legendary emperor Yao's son Danzhu 丹朱 was the feudal lord of Tang state (today's western Yi 翼 city, Shanxi) before it was later destroyed by King Cheng of Zhou.

Tang state was then granted to King Cheng's brother Shuyu 叔虞, after which the state name "Tang 唐" became the descendants' surname.

Danzhu's and Shuyu's descendants took Tang as their surname.

"I'm Danzhu's descendant. Surname Tang."

"I'm Shuyu's descendant. Surname Tang."

Legendary emperor Yao's descendant Xiefu 燮父 was given the southern part of Tang state (today's Tang town of north-western Sui county, Hubei). Hence his descendants' surname was "Tang 唐".

Famous Tang figure:

Ming Dynasty artist Tang Bohu 唐伯虎

Origins of the Surname Han 韩

Origins of the Surname Cao 曹

The surname "Cao" came about from three sources:
Legendary emperor Zhuanxu's 颛顼 grandson Luzhong 陆终 whose fifth son was named Cao An 曹安.

After King Wu of Zhou had overthrown the Shang Dynasty, he made his brother Shu Zhenduo 叔振铎 the ruler of Cao state. The state name "Cao 曹" then became his descendants' surname.

The people of Cao state (today's Samarkand of the Ozbek nationality, Xinjiang Uygur Autonomous Region) came to China and adopted the state name "Cao 曹" as their surname.

Famous Cao figures:

Three Kingdoms period politician Cao Cao 曹操

Three Kingdom period writer Cao Zhi 曹植 (son of Cao Cao)

Qing Dynasty novelist Cao Xueqin 曹雪芹, author of *Dream of Red Chamber*

Origins of the Surname Xu 许

One of legendary emperor Yandi's descendants was Boyi伯益. Boyi's descendant Wenshu文叔 was given the state of Xu许 (today's eastern Xuchang city, Henan).

Xu state was eliminated by Chu state, and the state name "Xu许" was carried by its later generations.

Famous Xu figures:

Eastern Han Dynasty ancient word study scholar Xu Shen许慎.

Modern China writer Xu Dishan许地山.

Origins of the Surname Deng 邓

There were two origins of surname "Deng":
The first origin dated back to the Xia Dynasty when there was a feudal state named "Deng 邓". Deng state was later destroyed by Chu state, and "Deng" was adopted as its descendants' surname.

Another origin came about during the Southern Tang kingdom of the Five Dynasties period. The last king Li Yu 李煜 had a son Li Congyi 李从镒 who was made the ruler of Deng state.

After the Southern Tang kingdom had fallen, his later generations escaped and used "Deng 邓" as their surname.

Famous Deng figures:

Qing Dynasty military governor Deng Shichang 邓世昌

Modern China political leader Deng Xiaoping 邓小平

Origins of the Surname Xiao 萧

Shang King Zhou had a brother named Wei Ziqi 微子启 who became the lord of Song state during the Western Zhou Dynasty.

Daxin 大心, a descendant of Wei Ziqi, was given the state of Xiao 萧 (today's north-western Xiao county, Anhui).

Xiao state was eliminated by Chu state, and the later generations had "Xiao 萧" as their surname.

Famous Xiao figure: Western Han Dynasty prime minister Xiao He 萧何

Bai白

During the time of Yandi, Bai Fu白阜 made a great contribution by regulating watercourses. Hence the later generations then adopted "Bai白" as surname. Moreover, during the Spring and Autumn period, Chu King Ping's grandchild Sheng胜 was assigned to Baiyu白羽 (today's Xixia county, Henan). His pseudonym was Baigong白公, also known as Bai Gongsheng白公胜. Bai Gongsheng later committed suicide after a rebellion. His descendants used "Bai" as their surname. Also, Jianshu of Qin state had a son named Bai Yibing白乙丙, and his descendants took "Bai" as surname.
Famous Bai figures:
Qin state well-known general Bai Qi白起,
Tang Dynasty great poet Bai Juyi白居易

Bai Juyi

Cheng程

Zhuanxu颛顼, the legendary emperor, assigned his two grandsons to govern Heaven and Earth. The elder grandson Zhong重 was in charge of offering sacrifices to Heaven while his younger brother Li黎 took care of earthly matters.
Zhong's offspring was later granted Cheng state (today's eastern Luoyang, Henan) during the Zhou Dynasty. His descendants then adopted "Cheng程" as their surname.
Famous Cheng figures:
Tang Dynasty great general Cheng Yaojin程咬金
Song Dynasty Neo-Confucian philosophers Cheng Hao程颢 and Cheng Yi程颐。

Chang常

During Huangdi's reign, there were two ministers named Chang Yi常仪 and Chang Xian常先. Chang Yi was in charge of moon divination and Chang Xian was the official responsible for engineering work. Thus their descendants' surname was "Chang".
Also, Qi state ruler Kangshu gave Chang state (today's south-eastern Teng county, Shandong) to his descendants and the later generations adopted the state name "Chang" as surname.
Famous Chang figures:
Tang Dynasty poet Chang Jian常建,
Ming Dynasty great general Chang Yuchun常遇春

The surname Chang常 is connected with the ancient Chinese fairy tale of "Chang E Flies to the Moon"!

The above mentioned Changyi, who performed the moon divination, was also said to be a concubine of Huangdi's great-grandson Emperor Ku. In the past, "仪" and "娥" sounded similar and were interchangeable, hence Chang E was possibly the embodiment of Changyi!

Dong Feng

Dong董
Dongfu董父, a descendant of legendary emperor Huangdi, was an official during legendary emperor Yushun's reign. He supposedly knew how to train a dragon to dance. Yushun conferred the surname "Dong董" on him. Also, during the Spring and Autumn period, Jin state's court historians were addressed as "Dong Shi董史", and their descendants would use this official title as their surname.
Famous Dong figures:
Spring and Autumn period Jin state's court historian Dong Hu董狐,
Han Dynasty great Confucian scholar Dong Zhongshu董仲舒,
Three Kingdoms period well-known physician Dong Feng董奉

Duan段

During the Spring and Autumn period, Duke Zhuang of Zheng's brother Gong Shuduan共叔段 planned to seize the throne but failed and fled to Gong共 (today's Hui county, Henan). His descendants were scattered everywhere and some carried the surname "Duan". Moreover, during the Western Jin Dynasty, the Xianbei minority also bore the surname of "Duan".
Famous Duan figures:
Tang Dynasty minister Duan Xiushi段秀实,
Tang Dynasty naturalist Duan Chengshi段成式

> Those with surnames Du杜 and Fan范 are the descendants of ancient China's legendary emperor Yao.

Du杜

The later generations of ancient China legendary emperor Yao's (also called Tang Yao) descendant Liu Lei刘累 had "Tangdu唐杜" as their surname. King Cheng of Zhou defeated Tang state and assigned the Tangdu families to the state of Du杜 (today's Xi'an city, Shaanxi). Some of their descendants used "Du" as surname. In addition, there were many national minorities who had had their surnames changed to Du杜, including the Xianbei nationality surname of Guduhun孤独浑 during the Northern Wei kingdom, Tushan徒单 of the Nüzhen nationality during the Northern Song Dynasty, Manchurian Eight Banners' surname善 and Tuketan图克坦 during the Qing Dynasty.

Du Fu

Famous Du figures:
Tang Dynasty great poets Du Fu杜甫 and DuMu杜牧

Fan范

A descendant of Emperor Yao moved to the state of Du杜 (today's Xi'an, Shaanxi) during the Zhou Dynasty and he was addressed as "Dubo杜伯". Dubo was killed and his son escaped to Jin state to become a general and was granted the state of Fan范 (today's Fan county, Henan). "Fan范" thus became the surname of his descendants.
Famous Fan figures:
Spring and Autumn period senior official of Yue state Fan Li范蠡,
Southern and Northern Dynasties philosopher Fan Zhen范缜,
Northern Song Dynasty official cum writer Fan Zhongyan范仲淹

Fu傅

There are two accounts describing the origin of the surname "Fu傅": Huangdi's descendant Da You大由 was assigned to Fu state. Hence the later generations had used "Fu" as surname. Another account was that Shang King Wuding's prime minister Shuo说(ancient pronunciation "yue悦") had toiled at building walls in Fuyan傅岩(today's south-eastern Pinglu county, Shanxi). Thus he was named Fu Shuo傅说 and his offspring then used "Fu傅" as surname.

Famous Fu figures:
LateMingtoearlyQingDynastymiracle-working physician Fu Shan傅山, Modern China translator Fu Lei傅雷

Fang方

It was said that legendary emperor Yandi's ninth-generation grandson, whose surname was Fanglei方雷, had won a battle achievement, thus Huangdi assigned him toMount Fang方山(aroundMount Song嵩山, north-central Henan) to set up a feudal state. Some of Fanglei's descendants then adopted "Fang方" as surname. Also, Huangdi had married a woman of surname Fanglei. She and his three other wives gave birth to 25 sons, one of whom was given the surname "Fang".

Fang Xiaoru

Famous Fang figures:
Ming Dynasty minister Fang Xiaoru方孝孺, Qing Dynasty writer Fang Bao方苞

Lei雷

The surname Lei雷 also originates from "Fanglei方雷" with some of the latter's descendants adopting the surname "Lei". Huangdi's subject Leigong had good medical skills and descendants took "Lei" as their surname. The surname "Lei" also originated from other nationalities who had altered their original surnames such as Chunlei春雷 of the Jingpo景颇nationality and Buke布柯 of the Jinuo基诺 nationality
adopting the Chinese surname "Lei雷" instead.

Famous Lei figures:
Qing Dynasty well-known physician Lei Dasheng雷大升, Qing Dynasty writer Lei Duo雷铎

Some surnames seem to have no connection with one another, but tracing back to their roots, they may have originated from the same family!

Fang方 and Lei雷 have their origins from surname "Fanglei方雷". Surnames Gong龚 and Hong洪 originate from surname "Gonggong共工" of ancient China!

Gong龚

Originally used as surname "Gong共". Tyrant King Li of the Western Zhou Dynasty was driven out by the people, and Gong Bohe共伯和 became the ruler. Bohe later gave the political power back to King Li's son Jing and returned to Gong state. The surname of Bohe's descendants was then named "Gong共" but was later changed to "Gong龚". Another account was that some descendants of Gonggong, a descendant of Yandi, began using the single character "Gong共" as their surname but later added the character "Long龙" to it in order to avoid enmity. Their surname thus became "Gong龚".

Famous Gong figures:
Han Dynasty Prefect of the Bohai Sea Gong Sui龚遂,
Qing Dynasty thinker cum writer Gong Zizhen龚自珍

Hong洪

The surname "Hong洪" originates from "Gonggong共工" of ancient China also. In ancient China, Gonggong, a descendant of Yandi, was an expert at regulating rivers and held an official position to manage irrigation works, thereby becoming known as Water God. During Shun's reign, Great Yu was sent to control floods, but Gonggong did not cooperate, so the latter was banished to the wilds in Jiangnan. In commemoration of their ancestor as Water God, Gonggong's descendants then added the character component of water to "Gong共", forming "Hong洪" as their surname. Moreover, some descendants of Gong Bohe共伯和 had also changed their surname to "Hong洪".

Famous Hong figures:
Qing Dynasty leader of the Taiping Heavenly Kingdom Hong Xiuquan洪秀全,
Qing Dynasty dramatist Hong Sheng洪升

Hong Xiuquan

Gu Kaizhi

Gu顾

The people with surname "Kunwu昆吾" during the Xia Dynasty had descendants who were assigned to the state of Gu (today's south-eastern Fan county, Henan). Gu state was wiped out by Shang Dynasty founder Cheng Tang, and Gu's descendants used their state name as surname. In addition, the Yue King Goujian of the Spring and Autumn period had a descendant who later became the Lord of Gu during the Han Dynasty and established his capital at Huiji会稽 (today's Shaoxing, Zhejiang). This person's descendants adopted his rank title "Gu顾" as their surname.

Famous Gu figures:
Eastern Jin Dynasty artist Gu Kaizhi顾恺之,
Ming-Qing Dynasty thinker Gu Yanwu顾炎武

Hao郝

During the Shang Dynasty, King Yi granted the state of Hao 郝 (today's Taiyuan, Shanxi) to Qi期, who was the son of his minister Hao Gu 郝骨. The later generations then used the conferred state name "Hao" as their surname. In addition, the Quhuan乌桓 nationality also had the surname of "Hao郝".
Famous Hao figures:
Song Dynasty medical scientist Hao Yun郝允,
Qing Dynasty classics scholar Hao Yixing郝懿行

Hou侯

During the Spring and Autumn period, Marquis Min of Jin晋潘侯 was driven off by its ruler Duke Wu. His descendants bore the surname "Hou侯". In addition, during the Northern Wei kingdom era, the Xianbei nationality surnames of Hounu侯奴 and Kehou渴侯 were changed to "Hou 侯".

Hou Fangyu

Famous Hou figures:
Late Ming Dynasty scholar Hou Fangyu 侯方域,
Late Ming Dynasty patriot Hou Tongzeng 侯垌曾

Jia 贾

During the Zhou Dynasty, King Kang granted the state of Jia 贾 (today's Linfen临汾, Shanxi) to Tang Shuyu's son Gongming公明. Jia state was eliminated by Jin state, with Gongming's descendants bearing the surname "Jia贾". Jia state was later given to Ji Ta季他 who was also known as Jia Ji贾季. Jia Ji was defeated by minister Zhao Dun when both vied for power, and the former's descendants adopted "Jia贾" as surname.

Jia Yi

Famous Jia figures:
Western Han Dynasty official cum writer Jia Yi贾谊,
Tang Dynasty poet Jia Dao贾岛

Jiang 江

Surname "Jiang" came from legendary emperor Zhuanxu's descendant Boyi. The latter had been assigned to the state of Jiang江 (today's south-western Zhengyang, Henan) which was wiped out by Chu state during the Spring and Autumn period. The later generations of Jiang state then took "Jiang江" as surname.

Famous Jiang figures:
Southern Dynasties period writer Jiang Yan江淹,
Southern Song Dynasty artist Jiang Can江参

Jin 金

The descendants of Huangdi's son Shao Hao少昊 whose surname was also known as "Jintian金天" adopted "Jin金" as their surname.

In addition, during the Western Han Dynasty, Xiongnu King Xiutu's crown prince had pledged allegiance to the Han emperor, and the latter bestowed on him the surname "Jin金". Hence his name was Jin Midi金日䃅, and his later generations had "Jin" as surname.

Jin Midi

Famous Jin figures:
Late Ming to early Qing Dynasty literary critic Jin Shengtan金圣叹,
Qing Dynasty calligrapher cum artist Jin Nong金农

The well-known military advisor Jiang Ziya 姜子牙 (Jiang Taigong) was a descendant of Emperor Yandi. Many surnames then came about from "Jiang 姜". Here are some examples.

Jiang 姜

Throughout history, due to varied reasons, many of emperor Yandi's descendants had had their surname changed. But later, Boyi made a contribution by assisting Great Yu in regulating rivers, for this he was allocated to Lü (today's Nanyang county, Henan) and was bestowed the ancestral surname of "Jiang 姜".

Famous Jiang figures:
Western Zhou Dynasty minister Jiang Taigong 姜太公,
Three Kingdoms period great general of the Shu kingdom Jiang Wei 姜维

Lü 吕

Empress Lü Zhi

Surname "Lü 吕" is also derived from Emperor Yandi's surname "Jiang 姜". Jiang Ziya 姜子牙 was also called Lü Shang 吕尚. Boyi did a great service to Xia Dynasty founder Great Yu by regulating rivers. He was granted the state of Lü 吕. The state was destroyed by Chu state during the Spring and Autumn period. The later generations then used the state name of "Lü 吕" as their surname. Some national minorities' surnames were also changed to "Lü 吕".

Famous Lü figures:
Qin state prime minister Lü Buwei 吕不韦
Han Dynasty empress Lü Zhi 吕雉

Ding 丁

During the Western Zhou Dynasty, Jiang Ziya (Jiang Taigong) had rendered great service by assisting Zhou King Wu to overthrow the Shang Dynasty. Hence he was assigned to Qi state and became known as Qi Taigong. His son Ji had been given the posthumous name of "Duke Ding of Qi齐丁公" after his death. His descendants thus used "Ding丁" as surname. During the Spring and Autumn period, the descendants of senior official Duke Ding of Song state also adopted "Ding丁" as surname.

Jiang Ziya

Famous Ding figures:
Han Dynasty inventor Ding Huan丁缓,
Qing Dynasty admiral Ding Ruchang丁汝昌

Cui崔

Jizi季子, son of Duke Ding of Qi of the Western Zhou Dynasty, gave the throne to his younger brother and moved to the state of Cui (today's north-western Zhangqiu章丘county, Shandong). Jizi's descendants then adopted "Cui" as surname. During the Western Jin Dynasty, "Cui" was one of the four major surnames of "崔(Cui)卢(Lu)王(Wang)谢(Xie)".

Famous Cui figures:
Tang Dynasty poets Cui Hao崔颢 and Cui Hu崔护

Lu卢

Duke Wen of Qi齐文公 who lived during the Spring and Autumn period was a descendant of Jiang Ziya. During the Spring and Autumn period, his grandson Xi was granted the state of Lu 卢(today's south-western Changqing county, Shandong). "Lu" then became the surname of his descendants.

Famous Lu figures:
Tang Dynasty poets Lu Zhaolin卢照邻 and Lu Lun卢纶

Qiu邱

Also written as "Qiu丘". During the Western Zhou Dynasty, Jiang Taigong of Qi state had some descendants who lived in Yingqiu营丘, so "Qiu丘" became their surname. Qing Dynasty Emperor Yongzheng later changed "Qiu丘" to "Qiu邱" in order to avoid the name taboo of the sage Confucius whose name was "Qiu丘".
Famous Qiu figures:
Song Dynasty anti-Jin general Qiu Huan邱奂,
Yuan Dynasty Taoist leader Qiu Chuji邱处机

Qiu Chuji

He贺

Duke Huan of Qi 齐桓公 was Jiang Taigong's descendant. During the Spring and Autumn period, he had a descendant named Qi Qingfu齐庆父. His later generations then used "Qing庆" as surname. During the Eastern Han Dynasty, in order to avoid the name taboo of Han Emperor Andi's father Liu Qing刘庆, the surname "Qing庆" was then changed to its synonym "He贺".
Famous He figures:
Tang Dynasty poet He Zhizhang贺知章,
Sui Dynasty great general He Ruobi贺若弼

Kong孔

Surname "Kong孔" came about from many sources. Huangdi had an official named Kong Jia孔甲. The latter's descendants then adopted "Kong" as surname. Cheng Tang成汤 of the Shang Dynasty whose name was "Lü履" and courtesy name "Taiyi太乙" had descendants who added the character "Zi子" to "Yi乙", forming the character "Kong孔" as their surname. During the Spring and Autumn period, Song state chief minister Zheng Kaofu's son Jia嘉 (courtesy name "Kongfu孔父") was killed. His son fled to Lu state and used Jia's name "Kong孔" as surname.

Famous Kong figures:
Spring and Autumn period great philosopher Confucius孔子,
Qing Dynasty dramatist Kong Shangren孔尚任

About Confucius: Kongzi, named Qiu with courtesy name Zhongni, was the founder of the Confucian school. He advocated ruling with benevolence and placed strong emphasis on moral development. His philosophy and teachings later greatly influenced later generations. Kongzi was also a great educator who felt that everyone should be given an equal opportunity to receive education. He advocated educating one according to his natural ability. He was later also addressed as the Most Sagely Master.

Kongzi's temple, cemetery and mansion are located at Qufu city in Shandong province. The main temple of Confucius was built in 478 BC to commemorate Kongzi. The cemetery contains Kongzi's tomb and the remains of his descendants. It is so far the largest and oldest clan cemetery. The Kong Family Mansion has also been called "The World's First Family". It has been the permanent home to Kongzi's direct line of descendants.

> Kongzi, the great philosopher and founder of the Confucian school during ancient China, and Mengzi, the "Lesser Sage" of the Confucian school, have surnames Kong孔 and Meng孟 respectively. These surnames are still carried by many people and are among the 100 major surnames.

Meng孟

The founder of Lu state was Zhou Gongdan's eldest son Boqin, Zhou Gongdan being the son of Zhou King Wen; Wei state's earliest ancestor was Kangshu who was also Zhou King Wen's son. Hence the Mengs are the offspring of Zhou King Wen's descendants who were of surname Ji姬. During the Spring and Autumn period, Duke Huan of Lu's son Qingfu庆父 murdered his father. His descendants changed their surname to "Mengsun孟孙" which was later shortened to "Meng孟". The descendants of Mengzhi孟絷 who was the elder brother of Duke Ling of Wei state also adopted "Meng孟" as their surname.

Famous Meng figures:
Warring States period Confucian philosopher Mencius孟子,
Tang Dynasty poet Meng Haoran孟浩然

About Mencius: Mengzi, named Ke, was another representative figure of the Confucian school. Known as the Lesser Sage, Mengzi was the most famous Confucian after Confucius himself. Mengzi advocated benevolent governance wherein the citizens were above the ruler, and that the latter will only gain the former's respect with his good morals. Mengzi also advocated the innate goodness of human nature. The most famous hall name of surname Meng is "Sanqiantang三迁堂(Hall of Three Shifts)", derived from the story of "Mencius's Mother Shifted Thrice". Mengzi's mother moved the family three times in order that her son would have an ideal environment conducive for learning and growth. At first, they lived near a cemetery and Mengzi would learn about tombs and wailing at funerals. His mother then shifted to live near the marketplace and Mengzi would learn to shout like the hawkers. Finally, Mengzi's mother moved and settled besides a school. Mengzi then learned to read and study like the scholars.

Liao廖

Legendary emperor Zhuanxu's descendant Shu An叔安 was granted the state of Liao. Thus his later generations adopted "Liao廖" as surname. In addition, the descendants of Zhou King Wen's son Boliao伯廖 also used "Liao" as surname.
Famous Liao figures:
Three Kingdoms period general of the Shu kingdom Liao Hua廖化,
Qing Dynasty writer Liao Yan廖燕

Long龙

Surname "Long龙" originated from the Yulong御龙 descendants. For example, Xia Dynasty's Yulong Liulei御龙刘累 had descendants with the surname "Long".
Famous Long figures:
Warring States period wise man Long Shu龙叔 and one of Xiang Yu's four well-known generals Long Qie龙且

Lu陆

Legendary emperor Zhuanxu's great-grandson Zhong终 was assigned to Luxiang陆乡. Hence his descendants' surname was "Lu陆". Moroever, during the Warring States period, Qi King Xuan's youngest son Ji Da季达 was given the state of Lu, and his descendants used the state name "Lu" as surname. In addition, monarch Xiao Wendi of the Northern Wei kingdom changed the Xianbei minority's surname "Bulugu步陆孤" to "Lu陆".

Lu You

Famous Lu figures:
Three Kingdoms period well-known general Lu Xun陆逊,
Southern Song Dynasty patriotic poet Lu You陆游

Niu牛

During the Western Zhou Dynasty, Song state's minister of justice (Sikou司寇) Niu Fu牛父 managed to resist attacks from the nomadic nationality Changdi but lost his life in the process. Niu Fu's descendants then used "Niu牛" as their surname.
Famous Niu Figures:
Sui Dynasty writer Niu Hong牛弘,
Song Dynasty anti-Jin general Niu Gao牛皋

> The Peng 彭 and Qian 钱 families are of the same family. Both are the descendants of Peng Zu!

Peng Zu

Peng 彭

Peng Zu 彭祖, a descendant of legendary emperor Zhuanxu 颛顼, was a famous figure of longevity who lived for 800 years. It was said that he was so good at cooking wild chicken and soup that he won the admiration of Emperor Yao and was thus granted the state of Peng (today's Xuzhou, Jiangsu). His later generations then bore the state name "Peng 彭" as their surname.

Famous Peng figures:
Western Han Dynasty great general Peng Yue 彭越
Modern China military leader Peng Dehuai 彭德怀.

Qian 钱

Legendary emperor Zhuanxu's grandchild Peng Zu 彭祖 was a well-known figure of longevity. Peng Zu's grandson Peng Fu 彭孚 became a chief monetary official. His descendants used his official title as their surname.

Famous Qian figures:
Five Dynasties' King Yue of Wu, Qian Liu 钱镠,
Tang Dynasty poet Qian Qi 钱起

Qin秦

Legendary Emperor Yao's minister Gao Tao皋陶 had a sixteenth-generation grandson Feizi非子 who was good at rearing livestock. Hence King Xiao of Zhou granted him the land of Qingu秦谷 (today's south-western Tianshui, Gansu). Feizi's descendants then used "Qin秦" as their surname. Moreover, the Duke of Zhou's son Boqin was given Lu state, and his descendants who were royals or bureaucrats were later assigned to Qin (today's northern Fan county, Henan), adopting Qin as surname.

Qin Yueren

Famous Qin figures:
Warring States period well-known physician Qin Yueren秦越人,
Northern Song Dynasty poet Qin Guan秦观,
Ming Dynasty female military governor Qin Liangyu秦良玉

> Those with the surname "Ren任" or "Xue薛" are descendants of Huangdi's son.

Ren任

Huangdi's young son Yuyang禹阳 was given the state of Ren (today's Jining济宁 county, Shandong). Hence his descendants took "Ren任" as surname.
Famous Ren figures:
Qing Dynasty artists Ren Weichang任渭长 and Ren Bonian任伯年

Xue薛

There were many accounts on the origin of surname "Xue薛". One origin of "Xue" comes from the surname "Ren任". Huangdi's son Yuyang was given Ren state. Thus "Ren任" was used as his surname. Great Yu assigned Yuyang's twelfth-generation grandson Xizhong奚仲to the state of Xue (today's Xue city, Shandong). Thus his descendants' surname was "Xue".
Famous Xue figures:
Tang Dynasty great general Xue Rengui薛仁贵,
Tang Dynasty female poet Xue Tao薛涛

Shao邵

During the Spring and Autumn period, surnames "Shao邵" and "Shao召" were considered to be the same surname. People with the surname Shao are the descendants of Duke Shao of Zhou 周召公 who was born of Zhou King Wen's concubine. He was given the state of Shao召 (today's north-western Qishan岐山, Shaanxi), and his descendants used state name "Shao" as surname.

Famous Shao figures:
Northern Song Dynasty philosopher Shao Yong邵雍,
Ming Dynasty artist ShaoMi邵弥

Shi施

Duke Hui of the Eastern Zhou Dynasty had a son whose name was Gongzi Wei公子尾 and courtesy name Shifu施父. Gongzi Wei's son Shibo施伯 used his father's courtesy name as surname. Hence the later generations had their surname as "Shi施".

Famous Shi figures:
Spring and Autumn period disciple of Confucius, Shi Zichang施子常,
Ming Dynasty author of the novel *Water Margin*, Shi Naian施耐庵

Shi Naian

Shi石

During the Spring and Autumn period, Duke Zhuang of Wei's minister Shi Que石碏 had rendered service to the state of Wei卫. Thus he was made a minister of Wei state, and his offspring adopted "Shi石" as surname.

Famous Shi figures:
Warring States period astronomer Shi Shen石申,
Song Dynasty great general Shi Shouxin石守信

Shi史

During the Zhou Dynasty, Zhou state's shiguan史官or court historian Yinyi尹佚 was a model for others. His descendants then adopted Yinyi's official title "Shi史"as their surname. In addition, those with surname "Ashina阿史那" during the Tang Dynasty had changed it to surname "Shi史". Another origin of surname "Shi"came from Huangdi's court historian Cang Jie仓颉. The latter's descendants had their surname as "Shi史".

Famous Shi figures:
Northern Song Dynasty well-known physician Shi Kan史堪,
Late Ming Dynasty minister Shi Kefa史可法

Su 苏

Legendary emperor Zhuanxu's descendant Kun Wu昆吾 was given the state of Su苏 (today's north-western Jiyuan济源 county, Henan). Thus his descendants used "Su" as their surname. In addition, during Northern Wei Dynasty Emperor Xiaowen's reign, the Xianbei minority's surname "Bolüe拔略" was changed to "Su苏".
Famous Su figures:
Western Han Dynasty minister Su Wu苏武,
Song Dynasty eminent poet Su Shi苏轼

Su Shi

Su Wu

Tan 谭

The state of Tan 谭(today's western Zhangqiu章丘 county, Shandong) during the Zhou Dynasty was the feudal state of Boyi's descendants. It was later destroyed by Qi state, and the people of Tan used state name "Tan谭" as surname.
Famous Tan figures:
Ming Dynasty well-known general Tan Lun谭纶 who fought the Japanese.
Tan Sitong谭嗣同, one of the "Six Gentlemen of the ReformMovement" during the late Qing Dynasty.

Wang 汪

There were two accounts on surname "Wang": During the Xia and Shang Dynasties, there existed a country called "Wangmang汪芒". Its countrymen had their surname as "Wangmang" at first but later it became a single character surname "Wang汪"; Another account came from Duke Cheng of Lu's son who was granted Wang state during the Spring and Autumn period. His descendants used the state name "Wang" as surname.
Famous Wang figures:
Song Dynasty poet Wang Yuanliang汪元量,
Yuan Dynasty naval navigator Wang Dayuan汪大渊

Wei 韦

Legendary emperor Zhuanxu's descendant Yuan Zhe元哲 was given the state of Shiwei豕韦 (today's south-eastern Hua滑 county, Henan), and his descendants took "Wei韦" as surname. In addition, when Western Han Dynasty great general Han Xin韩信 was killed, his son went into hiding in Nanyue. The character component "Wei韦" derived from the word "Han韩" was adopted as surname.
Famous Wei figures:
Tang Dynasty poet Wei Yingwu韦应物,
Five Dynasties' Former Shu kingdom poet Wei Zhuang韦庄

Wu武

Its origins came from several sources. One originated from Zhou King Ping's young son whose palm formed the character of "Wu武" when he was born, thus it became his surname. Another source said that during the Spring and Autumn period, Duke Dai of Song's son had a posthumous name "Wu武". His descendants then adopted it as surname. It was also said that there existed the Wuluo武罗 state, hence "Wu武" was used as a surname.

Famous Wu figures:
Tang Dynasty Empress Wu Zetian武则天,
Late Qing Dynasty philanthropist Wu Xun武训 who established free schools.

Wu Zetian

Xiong熊

The surname of Huangdi was also known as "Xiong熊". Thus his descendants also bore the surname of "Xiong". Moreover, Zhou King Wen's teacher was named Yu Xiong鬻熊. Thus his descendants took their ancestor's name "Xiong熊" as surname.

Famous Xiong figures:
Tang Dynasty poet Xiong Jiao熊皎,
Ming Dynasty great general Xiong Yanbi熊延弼

Surname Xia comes from Yu.

Great Yu

Xia夏

Great Yu had rendered great service by regulating rivers, thus Emperor Shun put him in charge of the country. After Yu's death, his son Qi启 established the Xia Dynasty although he was named as the founder. The last Xia Dynasty emperor Jie桀, who was a tyrant, was overthrown by Shang Tang商汤. The later generations bore the country name "Xia夏" as their surname.

Famous Xia figures:
Song Dynasty artist Xia Gui夏圭,
Late Ming Dynasty patriotic poet Xia Wanchun夏完淳

Yan严

During the Spring and Autumn period, Chu ruler Zhuang's descendants took his posthumous name of "Zhuang庄" as their surname. During the Eastern Han Dynasty, in order to avoid the taboo name of Han Emperor Mingdi or Liu Zhuang刘庄, surname "Zhuang庄" was changed to "Yan严".
Famous Yan figures:
Eastern Han Dynasty hermit Yan Guang严光,
Modern China thinker cum translator Yan Fu严复

Yan阎

King Wu of Zhou granted Taibo's great grandson Zhong Yi仲奕 the state of Yan阎. Thus "Yan" became the surname of his descendants. Zhou King Kang's son and Duke Cheng of Jin's son Yi懿 were once given the state of Yan阎. Their descendants later took state name "Yan" as surname.
Famous Yan figures:
Tang Dynasty great artist Yan Liben阎立本,
Qing Dynasty classics scholar Yan Ruoqu阎若璩

The Yao姚, Tian田 and Yuan袁 families are the descendants of Shun!

Shun

Yao姚

Legendary emperor Shun was born in the country of Yao姚 (today's southern Puyang county, Henan). Hence the later generations adopted "Yao" as surname. In addition, the people of Yao state during the Spring and Autumn period were Shang descendants, and their later generations adopted their state name "Yao" as surname. Other nationalities had switched to using "Yao" also. For e.g. the surname of Yao Gechong姚戈重, chief of the Qiang羌 nationality during Western Jin Dynasty, was originally "Xiqiangshaodang西羌烧当" during the Han Dynasty, but they claimed that they were emperor Shun's descendants and changed their surname to "Yao".
Famous Yao figures:
Tang Dynasty well-known prime minister Yao Chong姚崇,
Tang Dynasty historian Yao Silian姚思廉

Tian田

Chen Wan陈完, son of Duke Li of Chen state, was legendary emperor Shun's descendant Hu Gongman's tenth-generation grandson. During the Spring and Autumn period, he fled to Qi state when his country suffered internal chaos. Chen Wan then changed his surname to "Tian田" (ancient pronunciation of "Chen陈" and "Tian田" were similar). Another origin came about during the early Ming Dynasty, when minister Huang Zicheng was put to death by the Prince of Yan who later became Emperor Yongle. His descendants then switched to using "Tian田" as surname to avoid any misfortune. His later generations took "Tian" as surname as well.

Famous Tian figures:
Warring States period great general of Qi state Tian Dan田单
Modern China dramatist 田汉Tian Han

Yuan Chonghuan

Yuan袁

Hu Gongman胡公满, a descendant of legendary emperor Shun, was a chief minister during the Zhou Dynasty and he was given the state of Chen. He had a descendant Zhu诸 whose courtesy name was "Boyuan伯爰". Zhu's grandson took Zhu's courtesy name "Yuan爰" as his surname. In the ancient times, "Yuan爰" and "Yuan袁" were interchangeable.

Famous Yuan figures:
Ming Dynasty well-known general Yuan Chonghuan袁崇焕
Qing Dynasty poet Yuan Mei袁枚

Ye叶

During the Spring and Autumn period, Chu state's minister of war Shen Yinxu沈尹戌 died in a battle with Wu state. The Chu ruler put his son Shen Zhuliang沈诸梁 in charge of Ye state (today's Ye county, Henan), and he was named as Yegong叶公(Duke Ye)". A rebellion later erupted in Chu state and Yegong suppressed it. Yegong's descendants then adopted "Ye" as surname.

Famous Ye figures:
Song Dynasty poet Ye Mengde叶梦得,
Qing Dynasty well-known physician Ye Tianshi叶天士

Yin尹

In ancient China, Shaohao's son was granted Yin尹 city (today's north-eastern Xi隰 county, Shanxi). His descendants took the city's name as their surname. Moreover, during the Shang and Zhou Dynasties, there was an official title of "Yin尹", and descendants of these officials would use the official title as their surname.
Famous Yin figures:
Han Dynasty historian Yin Gengshi尹更始,
Northern Song Dynasty poet Yin Zhu尹洙

Yu余

During the Spring and Autumn period, there lived a senior official named You Yu由余in Qin state. His ancestors were the people of Jin state. They lived in the western regions to avoid turmoil. You Yu later resided in Qin state as an envoy and rendered a great service by assisting Duke Mu. You Yu's descendants later adopted his name "Yu" as their surname
Famous Yu figures:
Southern Song Dynasty well-known general Yu Jie余玠 who fought against the Mongolians.
Qing Dynasty writer Yu Huai余怀

Zeng Can

Zeng曾

Shaokang少康, the fifth king of the Xia Dynasty, assigned his youngest son Qulie曲烈 to be the lord of the state of Zeng鄫(today's north-western Cangshan苍山 county, Shandong) which was overthrown by Ju state during the Spring and Autumn period. The crown prince fled to Lu state, having "Zeng鄫" as his surname, but Zeng鄫 was later changed to Zeng曾.
Famous Zeng figures:
Zeng Can曾参, disciple of Confucius
Qing Dynasty governor of Jiangxi and Jiangsu provinces Zeng Guofan曾国藩

Zhong钟

During the Shang Dynasty when King Zhou纣 ruled, his brother Qi启 was granted the state of Wei微. After King Wu of the Zhou Dynasty had destroyed the Shang Dynasty, Qi was given Song state and addressed as Duke Huan of Song. During the Spring and Autumn period, his great-grandson Bozong伯宗 who was an official of the Jin state was killed. Bozong's son Zhouli州犁 travelled to Zhongli 钟离 (today's Fengyang, Anhui) in Chu state. Boli's later generations then used "Zhong钟" as surname.

Famous Zhong figures:
Three Kingdoms period calligrapher Zhong You钟繇,
Southern Dynasties period literary critic Zhong Rong钟嵘

Zou邹

During the Spring and Autumn period, Song state's minister Zheng Kaofu正考夫 was granted the state of Zou邹 (today's Zou county, Shanxi). Thus his descendants had "Zou" as their surname.

Famous Zou figures:
Warring States period Qi state minister Zou Ji邹忌,
Ming Dynasty Neo-Confucian philosopher Zou Shouyi邹守益

Dai戴

Surname "Dai" originated from two sources: One came from the people of Dai state (today's eastern Minquan, Henan) during the Western Zhou Dynasty. Dai state was later destroyed by Song state, and "Dai戴" was used as surname by its descendants. Another origin came from Duke Dai of Song宋戴公. "Dai戴" was his shi hao谥号or posthumous name, and his descendants adopted his posthumous name as their surname.

Famous Dai figures:
Qing Dynasty philosopher Dai Zhen戴震,
Modern China poet Dai Wangshu戴望舒

King Wen of Zhou was a well-known benevolent ruler in Chinese history. Many surnames originated from him.

The surname of Zhou King Wen was Ji姬, and Ji originated from Huangdi, so he was the latter's descendant!

Cai蔡

The Cai ancestor was Shudu叔度, the younger brother of Zhou King Wu. After King Wu overthrew the Shang Dynasty, Shudu was made the lord of Cai state (today's south-western Shangcai上蔡, Henan) and was then addressed as Caishu蔡叔. Caishu worked with Wugeng武庚(a descendant of the Yin殷 people) and rose in rebellion. But both were suppressed and banished by the Duke of Zhou. Caishu's son later became Cai's ruler. After Cai state was destroyed by Chu state during the Spring and Autumn period, the state name "Cai蔡" became the surname of its descendants.

Cai Lun

Famous Cai figures:
Han Dynasty inventor of paper Cai Lun蔡伦
Han Dynasty female writer Cai Wenji蔡文姬

Feng冯

Bi Gonggao毕公高, the fifteenth son of Zhou King Wen, had a descendant by the name of Bi Wan毕万. The latter was a senior official of Jin state during the Spring and Autumn period. He was put in charge of the state of Wei魏 (today's north-eastern Rui芮 city, Shanxi). Some of Bi Wan's descendants were given the state of Feng, so "Feng冯" was used as their surname.

Famous Feng figures:
Ming Dynasty novelist FengMenglong冯梦龙
Modern China warlord Feng Yuxiang冯玉祥

Kang Youwei

Zhou King Wen

Pan 潘

It originated from the Western Zhou imperial members. Ji Sun 季孙, the son of Bi Gonggao 毕公高, was enfeoffed as the lord of Pan state. The state's descendants then had "Pan 潘" as their surname. During the reign of Northern Wei emperor Xiao Wendi, he changed the Xianbei minority's surname "Poduoluo 破多罗" to become "Pan 潘".

Famous Pan figures:
Western Jin Dynasty writer Pan Yue 潘岳
Ming Dynasty irrigation expert Pan Jixun 潘季驯

Jiang 蒋

Boling 伯龄, the third son of the Duke of Zhou of the Western Zhou dynasty, was given the state of Jiang 蒋 (today's Jiang town of north-eastern Gushi 固始 county, Henan; another account places it at Guangshan county, Henan.) Jiang state was destroyed by Chu state during the Spring and Autumn period. The descendants' surname "Jiang 蒋" was derived from the state name.

Famous Jiang figures:
Qing dynasty poet Jiang Shiquan 蒋士铨
Modern China Chinese Nationalist leader Chiang Kai-shek 蒋介石

Kang 康

The surname "Kang" came about from two sources. A feudal lord of Wei state during the Spring and Autumn period was named Kangshu 康叔. His descendants later used his posthumous name "Kang" as their surname. Also in the Western Regions, the people of Kangju 康居 country settled in the Central Plains during the Han Dynasty, and their descendants used their country name "Kang 康" as surname.

Famous Kang figures:
Ming Dynasty dramatist Kang Hai 康海,
Late Qing Dynasty reform leader Kang Youwei 康有为

Lai赖
Lai state existed during the Spring and Autumn period, and its descendants adopted state name "Lai" as surname.
Famous Lai figures:
Ming Dynasty magistrate of Yuanjiang沅江 county Lai Li赖礼,
Qing Dynasty artist Lai Zhen赖珍

Mao毛
Zhou King Wen's son Bodan伯聃 was assigned to the state of Mao (today's Yiyang county, Henan), and his descendants used the state name as surname. Moreover, after Zhou King Wu had overthrown the Shang Dynasty, he gave his brother Shuzheng叔郑 the state of Mao (today's Mount Xiqi and Fufeng扶风, Shaanxi). The descendants later bore the surname "Mao".

Mao Zedong

Famous Mao figures:
Warring States period's Mao Sui毛遂 who volunteered his services.
Modern China's Chairman of the People's Republic of China Mao Zedong毛泽东

Shen沈
Zhou King Wen's tenth son Dan Shuji聃叔季 was granted the state of Shen沈 (today's northern Pingyu平舆 county, Henan) during Zhou King Cheng's reign. Shen state was later eliminated by Cai state, and "Shen沈" became the surname of the state's descendants.
Famous Shen figures:
Southern and Northern Dynasties writer Shen Yue沈约,
Northern Song Dynasty scientist Shen Kuo沈括

Wan万
During the Spring and Autumn period, Jin state minister Bi Wan's descendants took his name "Wan" as their surname.
Famous Wan figures:
Southern and Northern Dynasties musician of the Liang kingdom Wan Baochang万宝常,
Modern China dramatist Wan Jiabao万家宝 (also known as Cao Yu曹禺)

Wei 魏

During the Spring and Autumn period, Duke Xian of Jin assigned senior official Bi Wan to the state of Wei魏 (today's northern Rui芮 city, Shanxi). Hence Bi Wan's descendants used "Wei魏 " as surname.

Famous Wei figures:
Tang Dynasty well-known minister Wei Zheng魏征
Three Kingdoms period general of the Shu state Wei Yan魏延

Yu 于

During the Western Zhou Dynasty, Zhou King Wu's son was put in charge of Yu邘(today's Yu邘 town of northern Qinyang沁阳, Henan). The later generations dropped the right character component of "Yu邘" and used "Yu于" as their surname.

In addition, those having the surname of "Chunyu淳于" during the Tang Dynasty had it changed to surname "Yu于" in order to avoid the taboo name of Li Chun李纯 (Emperor Xianzong of Tang).

Famous Yu figures:
Ming Dynasty minister Yu Qian于谦
Qing Dynasty governor of the Jiangsu and Jiangxi provinces Yu Chenglong于成龙

Prominent Clan Names and Hall Names

In the past, some Chinese used to show prominent clan names such as "Taiyuan太原", "Xihe西河" on the front door of their houses. Such names would also be written on the red lanterns during a wedding or on the mourning lanterns during a funeral.

What does "Taiyuan太原" and "Xihe西河" represent?

That's the name of a prominent clan. We can also guess the surname of this family from their prominent clan name.

"Junwang郡望" refers to the respected clans of a county. Between the Spring and Autumn period and the Sui Dynasty, areas were divided into different local places of administration called jun郡. The name of a junwang was derived from the name of the place that was bestowed on one's clan ancestors or the place which one's illustrious ancestors had once lived in. Hence, a junwang name is a form of ancestral mark that suggests the origins of one's surname or the place of origin of one's clan.

Some surnames had several junwang names, and different surnames may be sharing the same junwang name. For example, the prominent clan name of surnames Han韩, Deng邓, Ye叶 and Bai白 is Nanyang南阳 (Nanyang, Henan).

What is a hall name then?

A tanghao堂号(hall name) refers to the name of one's ancestral hall. The Chinese enshrine and worship their ancestors' memorial tablets in an ancestral hall. Every family used to have an ancestral hall and they would give it a name. Hall names may also be used for shops, libraries, halls and on lanterns to indicate one's surname and clan. A junwang name can usually be used as a hall name. For example, the "Taiyuantang太原堂 (Hall of Taiyuan)" of Wang王 families, "Longxitang陇西堂(Hall of Longxi)" of Li李 families and "Pengchengtang 彭城堂 (Hall of Pengcheng)" of Liu刘 families.

Here are some of the junwang names that can be found.

Jingzhao京兆：Song宋, Du杜, Duan段, Shi史, Wei韦, Feng冯, Gao高, Che车, Kang康, Li黎, Yong雍, Zong宗, Shu舒, Pu浦, Huangfu皇甫

Taiyuan太原：Wang王, Hao郝, Guo郭, Huo霍, Wu武, Yan阎, Wu邬, Yi易, Shi师, Zhu祝, Wen温, Yuchi尉迟

Yingchuan颍川：Chen陈, Zhong钟, Lai赖, Tian田, Lu陆, Hu胡, Yuan袁, Wu邬, Han韩, Feng冯, Yu虞, Gan干, Wu乌

Runan汝南：Zhou周, Yuan袁, Liao廖, Yin殷, Lan蓝, Qi齐, Mei梅, Sheng盛, Ying应, Sha沙, Nan南

Henan河南：Fang方, Qiu邱, Lu陆, Mu穆, Chu褚, Yuan元, Li利, Gao高, Song宋, Pan潘, Liang梁, Zhu朱

Tianshui天水：Zhao赵, Qin秦, Yan严, Jiang姜, Yin尹, Zhuang庄, Pi皮, Gui桂, Qiang强, Shangguan上官, Liang梁

Fufeng扶风：Ma马, Wan万, Dou窦, Lu鲁, Ban班, Lu禄, Duan段, Su苏, Song宋

Nanyang南阳：Han韩, Deng邓, Ye叶, Bai白, Teng滕, Cen岑, Yue乐, Zhai翟

Pingyang平阳：Wang汪, Ji纪, Chai柴, Xie解, Wu巫, Qiu仇, Ou欧, Rao饶

Jiyang济阳：Jiang江, Ding丁, Tao陶, Zuo左, Ke柯, Yu庾, Bian卞

Hedong河东：Xue薛, L|吕, Wei卫, Liu柳, Pei裴, Pu蒲, Nie聂

Longxi陇西：Li李, Peng彭, Dong董, Guan关, Niu牛, Xin辛, Shi时

Wuxing吴兴：Shen沈, Yao姚, Shi施, Long龙, Shui水, Yu余, Ming明

Xihe西河：Lin林, Mao毛, Zhuo卓, Chi池, Bu卜, Zai宰, Jin靳

Anding安定：Liang梁, Hu胡, Cheng程, Wu伍, Meng蒙, Deng邓, Xi席

Bohai渤海：Gao高, Gan甘, Feng封, Ju居, Ouyang欧阳

Wuling武陵：Gong龚, Long龙, Gu顾, Hua华, An安, Ran冉

Chenliu陈留：Xie谢, Ruan阮, Yu虞, Tu屠, Yi伊, Yuan袁

Pengcheng彭城：Liu刘, Qian钱, Jin金, Chao巢, Cao曹, Yuan袁

Donghai东海：Xu徐, Qi戚, Zang臧, He何, Mao茅, Yu于

Zhongshan中山：Tang汤, Zhen甄, Jiao焦, Zhong仲

Fanyang范阳：Lu卢, Zou邹, Yan燕, Jian简

Qinghe清河：Zhang张, Fu傅, Bei贝, Fang房, Cui崔

Hongnong弘农：Yang杨, Diao刁, Mu牧, Feng冯

Peijun沛郡：Zhu朱, Liu刘, Xue薛

Pingyuan平原：Chang常, Wen温, Rui芮

Jiangxia江夏：Huang黄, Fei费

Xingyang荥阳：Zheng郑, Pan潘

Lean乐安：Sun孙, Jiang蒋

Lujiang庐江：He何, He河

Yanling延陵：Wu吴

Wugong武功：Su苏

Many junwang are shared by families of different surnames.

Genealogy

"My friend, our ancestors of 500 years ago might not be the same, although we share the same surname!"

"Exactly! A surname originates from many sources, while different surnames may share the same ancestor."

"But it has been eons, how can we know the origin of our own surname?"

"Look it up in the book of genealogy!"

A genealogical book records the data of different clans by surnames. It records the origins and development of each family surname. In the past, every family placed much importance on the updating of the book. During some dynasties, genealogical books were used as reference when selecting talents or officials, and arranging for marriage or funeral. Genealogy has had a long history. The inscriptions on bones of the Shang Dynasty were the earliest indication of simple genealogy.

Family Genealogy of Kong
The Kong 孔 family, originating from Qufu in Shandong, was also known as "The World's First Family". Its genealogy was considered to be of the longest span and the most complete one in the history of China. Since the Song Dynasty when the genealogy of Kong was established, its lineage had been continued in good order for the next 1,000 years. The Kong genealogy abided by some strict rules: foster son, son-in-laws who were married into the bride's family, monks and the disgraced ones were not included in the record. Also, any Kong member who went to serve as a servant would also have his surname changed and his name would not be recorded in the genealogical book.

Contents of a genealogical book

1. Surname's origin and development
The origins of the surname or the reason for alteration of surname are recorded.

2. Tanghao堂号 (Hall name)
A tanghao堂号 or hall name reflects the place where a surname has originated from. It suggests the connection between a surname and its patriarchal clan. It is an important lead for the later generations to trace the origins of their ancestry.

3. Shixibiao世系表 (Pedigree table)
It indicates the relationship among the members of the clan. It is a diagram that shows the name of every descendant of the clan, the clan ancestors and any famous figure who was from the clan.

4. Jiaxun 家训 (Family precepts)
The jiaxun家训 or family precepts are the standard rules for action for the clan members. It records many well-known sayings and aphorisms about home affairs management and education.

5. Jiazhuan家传 (Family biography)
It records the deeds of clan members who were reputable and had achievements.

6. Cultural compilation
It records the books, writings, letters or other works by the famous ones of the clan such as prints, portraits, calligraphy works and songs.

7. Genealogical pictures
They refer to old photographs of the clan, portrait of the deceased, and photos of the ancestral halls, tombs and former residence.

Part Two: Chinese Given Names

How do the Chinese choose given names? What naming customs are there? Find out the origin of given names, how names are selected, naming taboos and other interesting tidbits about names.

1. Origins of Given Names

Surnames serve as markers to identify different groups, and within groups, given names serve to identify individuals.

Pictograph: The ancient Chinese character "ming名(name)" is composed of the characters "xi夕(evening)" and "kou口(mouth)". This implies that one could hardly be seen clearly in the evening, and thus had to say out his name to make himself known to others.

2. Naming Traditions

There were already customs regarding naming during the Western Zhou Dynasty.

Ancient Naming Traditions

The father was not allowed in the confinement room for three months after the child's birth; he could only send people to ask after his wife and express concern.

Master asks Madam to rest more.

After three months, a naming ceremony would be held, attended by all the senior female members of the family, such as grandmothers and aunts.

Congratulations!

The mother would have a bath and change of clothes, and the baby's hair would be shaved, leaving only a section that would be tied in a pair of little horns.

How adorable!

The mother would then take the child out. The most senior female relative would look at the child and say:

Madam (Mother's surname) will take the child to see the father today.

Testing vocational inclinations

It was the fashion of the Han people and some minority groups to test a child's vocational inclination when the child turned one. A number of items, such as a bow and arrows, paper and brush, valuables, coins and toys would be set before the child, who would be allowed to pick one. The item selected in this way would be used to divine the child's inclinations and future vocation. A name might also be selected based on this item. For example, a child who picked a book may be called "Fond of Books钟书" or "Study习书", or if he grabbed a bow, he may be named "Long Bow长弓" or "Keen Arrow劲矢".

The famous writer Qian Zhongshu钱钟书 received his name in this way, as he grabbed a book when he was tested.

Weighing in a basket

This custom has its origins in Jiangnan, the region south of the Yangtze River. The parents weighed the child together with some lucky objects, such as a book, bamboo or even his father's shoes or mother's hair, and then named the child according to the weight, the greater the weight the better.

Stealing names

The new parents would ask a "name-stealer" to go to a flourishing household with many children and grandchildren to steal a pair of chopsticks and a bowl. The mother waited with the infant to "welcome" the name-stealer, who on seeing the child, called out "Little Chopsticks" or "Little Bowl". The mother would then reply on behalf of the baby, "Hey! Hey!"

Meeting surnames

Around Henan's Zhengzhou and Kaifeng regions, on the first morning of the child's birth, the father went out to "meet surnames". He would kowtow to the first person he encountered, whether man or woman, young or old, and ask the person to name the child.

This naming method is pretty dicey!

If the person so met named the child Manure or Piglet or Puppy, they would have to take it as given!

Poor No Dustpan

Third day wine
The Dong people of Sanjiang in Guangxi name their children three days after the birth. After the baby is passed around, the youths of the paternal family sing to ask the baby's aunt to name the child, and she also answers in song. Then everyone views and blesses the baby.

Divine naming with unhusked rice

The Bulang people of Yunnan use unhusked rice grains to determine the auspicious time for naming a child. During the naming ceremony, the person in charge throws eight rice grains. If the rice grains land in four pairs, it is considered auspicious and a name can be given immediately; if not, the rice grains are cast again until they land in the required four pairs.

Turning the bird's beak
Among the Luoba people in Tibet, the mother is the one who names the child. The family prepares the beak of a bird that has a pleasant call. During the naming ceremony, as the mother turns the beak in circles above the child's mouth, she silently recites a list of names chosen earlier, and the name she is reciting when the child expresses happiness is chosen.

Name what you see
For the Long people in the southwest of China, the father goes out on the day the child is born to look for a name. The first thing he encounters will be the child's name. For example, if he sees a swallow (yanzi), the child will be called Yanzisanmei (Third Sister Swallow), and if he sees a mountain goat (shanyang), the child will be called Yangsanmei (Third Sister Goat).

Hitting People for Names

3. How Names Are Chosen

It is written in the classic *Zuo Zhuan* from the early Qin Dynasty that there are six prohibitions in the matter of naming: "No Countries, No Official Ranks, No Mountains and Rivers, No Diseases, No Beasts, No Tools". As these are all common words, it seems disrespectful to apply them to people

Although the use of animal names was prohibited, people have been adopting domestic animals' names.

The wife of Han Dynasty emperor Liu Bang adopted a beast-like name "Lü Zhi吕雉". Zhi refers to pheasant.

Names recorded in the Jin Dynasty history book *Jinshi* include Fur Seal海狗, Donkey Li李瘤驴, Doggie Tang唐括狗儿, Piglet Wanyan完颜猪儿; the grandson of Jin Wushu was called Goat's Hoof羊蹄, and Hu Shahu's son was called Pig Dropping猪粪. The dynastic history book *Yuanshi* has records of names like Doggie Shima石抹狗狗, Pig-dog Ning宁猪狗 and Ugly Donkey丑驴.

Why was Duke Cheng of Jin called Black Bottom?

| Duke Cheng of Jin of the Spring and Autumn period was also known as "Black Bottom". But why would a state ruler adopt such a strange name? | It is said that when he was born, his mother had dreamt of a deity who painted the child's buttocks black. "This child with a black bottom will become a ruler in future." | Hence, he was named "Black Bottom" and later indeed became the ruler of Jin state. |

Methods of naming based on:

I. Birth situation
When Confucius' son was born, Duke Zhao of Lu happened to send him a liyu鲤鱼(carp). Hence, Kongzi named his son Kongli孔鲤.

II. Birthdate or birthplace
Emperor Qin Shihuang was born on New Year's Day during zhengyue正月(first month of the lunar year). As zheng正 and zheng政 were used interchangeably in ancient times, he was thus named Zheng政.

III. Unique appearance
As an infant, the crown of Confucius' head was depressed at the middle, while its surrounding area was raised. This shape resembled qiuling丘陵(hills), hence Confucius was named "丘".

IV. Parents' expectations
These would include names such as Guangzu光祖 (glory to ancestors), Chaoqun超群 (prominent), Shunfu顺富 (wealthy), and Guodong国栋 (country's pillar).

V. Reverence for a living person or admiration for a virtuous person in history
When Mengzong孟宗 was the Prefect of Yuzhang during the Three Kingdoms period, he was very popular among the common people. Thus, most people would name their children "Meng孟".

An opposite example would be Qin Hui秦桧. He was a treacherous official of the Southern Song Dynasty who caused general Yue Fei's death. Since then, practically nobody will use "Hui桧" in their names.

VI. Political situation and reform
From the establishment of new China to the Cultural Revolution, political situations had an influence on the way of naming: Zheng Jiefang郑解放 (liberation), Qin Jianguo秦建国 (building nation), Liu Jianshe刘建设 (build), Meng Yuejin孟跃进 (leap forward), Dong Wenge董文革 (Cultural Revolution) and Xing Weibing邢卫兵 (bodyguard).

VII. Moral ideals

The Chinese advocate virtues and like to adopt names such as Keqin克勤(industrious), Dehuai德怀 (with virtues), Shouli守礼(observe manners) and Shanglian尚廉(honour honesty).

VIII. Names of places

The name of writer Guo Moruo郭沫若 was derived from two hometown rivers, namely "Moshui沫水" (Dadu River) and "Ruoshui若水" (Yalong River).

Take note of name confusion

Homophonic: Many Chinese characters have similar pronunciations, thus do avoid adopting offensive homophonic characters when it comes to naming. Zhushi朱石 – Pig Droppings猪屎, Liao Yifu廖逸夫 – a pot of urine尿一壶, Jidan纪丹 hen's egg 鸡蛋, Zhou Yugang周玉刚 – smelly fish-tank臭鱼缸, Hu Lijing胡礼经 – vixen 狐狸精

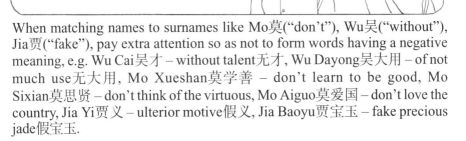

When matching names to surnames like Mo莫("don't"), Wu吴("without"), Jia贾("fake"), pay extra attention so as not to form words having a negative meaning, e.g. Wu Cai吴才 – without talent无才, Wu Dayong吴大用 – of not much use无大用, Mo Xueshan莫学善 – don't learn to be good, Mo Sixian莫思贤 – don't think of the virtuous, Mo Aiguo莫爱国 – don't love the country, Jia Yi贾义 – ulterior motive假义, Jia Baoyu贾宝玉 – fake precious jade假宝玉.

How the Famous Adopted Their Names

I. Emperor Tang Taizong (Li Shimin)

II. Li Bai

The great poet of Tang Dynasty, also known as "Poet Immortal", had a courtesy name called "Taibai太白". His name was actually derived from a dream.

In ancient China, Jinxing金星(Venus) was called Taibaixing 太白星, also known as Changgeng长庚 (Venus appearing in the western sky during evening) or Qiming启明(Venus appearing in the east sky before dawn).

Li Bai's mother dreamt of the Changgeng and gave birth to him.

This is an auspicious sign. I shall name him after the Taibaixing Venus!

Li Bai grew up and displayed extraordinary liteary talent like a poet immortal who had descended to earth.

Song Dynasty poet Ouyang Xiu wrote a poem that describes the "Taibai" (Li Bai) on earth as the "Taibai" (Venus) in heaven.

III. Su Shi and Su Zhe

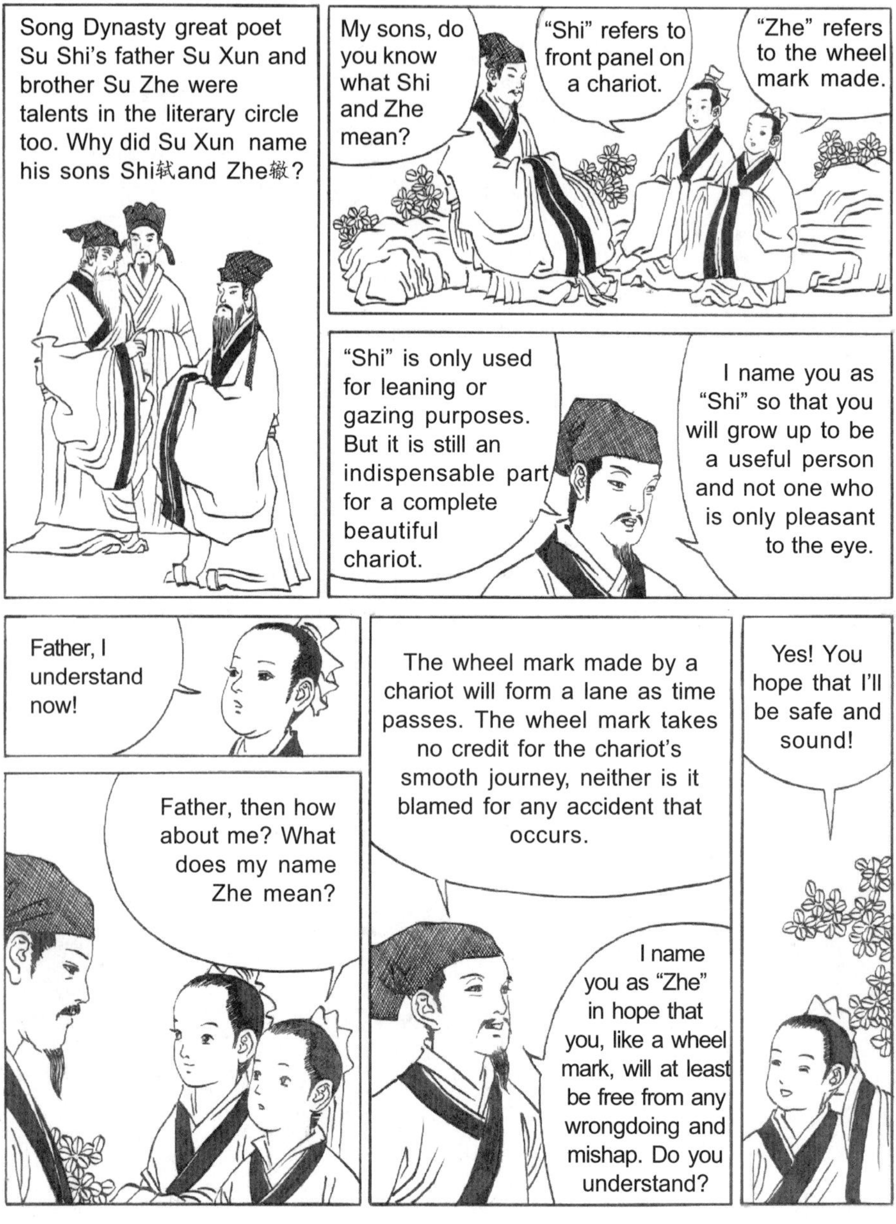

IV. Xu Beihong

The original name of Xu Beihong, a master painter of modern China, was Xu Shoukang.

Shoukang 寿康 carries good meaning of longevity and healthy.

Why was it changed to "Beihong" then?

This was because Xu Beihong came from a poverty-stricken family and never had the chance to receive a proper education. So, he was often treated coldly by others. In order to have a foothold in the society, he later decided to attend the "Yang Xuetang" foreign school.

But his father could not afford the money and Beihong had to borrow from others. He felt sad to see that how one was treated was dependent on whether one was successful or not. So he had his name changed to "Beihong 悲鸿", meaning sad swan.

Since then, his name served as an encouragement for him to diligently learn the art of painting.
Eventually, he became a great artist of his generation.

Commonly used names

The characters adopted for females are usually gentle in nature, used to express the female's beauty, gentleness, and good and refined moral character:

Character part with a "女"(female)
xian娴, na娜, shan姗, e娥, miao妙, wan婉, ting婷, juan娟, ni妮, chang嫦

Characters expressing virtues:
xian贤, hui慧, qiao巧, jie洁, qing清, xiu秀, zhen贞, shan善, shu淑, chun纯

Characters indicating looks and disposition:
ying盈, jing静, mei媚, mei美, qian倩, ya雅, ling灵, fen芬, fang芳

Characters related to flowers and birds:
lan兰, hua花, zhi芝, mei梅, lian莲, ju菊, li莉, feng凤, yan燕

Characters related to scenery:
yun云, yue月, chun春, qiu秋, xue雪, xia霞, hong虹

Characters referring to jewellery:
zhen珍, zhu珠, qiong琼, yao瑶, lin琳, ling玲, yu玉

As for male names, most characters have magnificent and majestic meaning to express masculinity:

Characters expressing virtues:
li礼, yi义, ren仁, lian廉, de德, qian谦, zheng正, qin勤, zhong忠, xin信

Characters expressing strength:
gang刚, qiang强, jian坚, zhi志, yi毅, xiong雄, hao豪, wei威, yong勇, wei伟

Characters indicating wealth and fortune:
cai财, fu富, wang旺, rong荣, fa发, fu福, shou寿, xing兴, sheng盛, sheng升

Characters indicating glory:
guang光, zong宗, yao耀, zu祖, hui辉, hao浩, chang昌, xian显, sheng胜, shi世

Characters indicating talents:
cai才, jie杰, jun俊, cong聪, ming明, zhi智, wen文, wu武, jian建, gong功

Common Character

In some families, a common character is used in each sibling's name. For example:

It is also possible to use a common character for names within the clan. These common clan characters were long decided by the ancestors of the family. The common characters for 12 generations or more can be stated at one go. With common clan characters, every member of the clan is given a name which corresponds to his rank (in terms of generation) in the clan.

Common characters of the Kong family

During the Qing Dynasty, Emperor Qianlong set down 30 common characters for Confucius and his descendants. A descendant, Kong Lingyi, later added another 20. These 50 common characters are listed in order from left to right as follows:

希	言	公	彦	承	宏	闻	贞	尚	衍
兴	毓	传	继	广	昭	宪	庆	繁	祥
令	德	维	垂	佑	钦	绍	念	显	扬
建	道	敦	安	定	懋	修	肇	益	常
裕	文	焕	景	瑞	永	锡	世	绪	昌

4. Characteristics of Naming Throughout the Ages

Shang Dynasty
Names were chosen based on ganzhi 干支 (the Heavenly Stems and Earthly Branches). E.g. Kong Jia孔甲, Wu Ding武丁 and Pan Geng盘庚, where Jia甲, Ding丁 and Geng庚 are the first, fourth and seventh of the ten Heavenly Stems respectively. There were names which indicated positions also, e.g. Wai Bing 外丙 (outside, third), Zhong Bing中丙 (center, third), Tai Jia太甲 (highest, first), Xiao Jia小甲 (young, first) and Nan Geng南庚 (south, seventh).

Spring and Autumn Period
People were fond of adding characters like "zhi之" or "zi子" as an auxiliary word in between the surname and given name. E.g. Zhu Zhiwu烛之武, Jie Zhitui介之推 and Wu Zixu伍子胥.

Han Dynasty and Three Kingdoms period
Many given names were single characters, e.g. Liu **Bang**, Zhang **Liang**, Han **Xin**, Xiao **He**, Cao **Cao**, Liu **Bei**, Sun **Quan**, Zhuge **Liang**, Zhang **Fei**, Guan **Yu**, Zhao **Yun** and Zhou **Yu**.

Wei, Jin, Southern and Northern Six Dynasties period
The use of character "zhi之" in names was popular during this era, e.g. Wang Xizhi王羲之, Wang Xianzhi王献之, etc.

Tang Dynasty
Most people liked using numerals in names which indicated seniority. E.g. Li Bai was Li Shier李十二 (Twelfth Li), Du Fu was Du Er杜二 (Second Du), Bai Juyi was Bai Ershier白二十二 (Twenty-second Bai), Han Yu was Han Shiba韩十八 (Eighteenth Han). The suggested seniority might not only be among family brothers, but might also include cousins, distantly related cousins or even uncles.

Five Dynasties
The character "yan彦" was a popular choice in naming, e.g. Yanzhang彦章, Yanchang彦昌.

5. Names of Commoners in Ancient Times

In the past, ordinary people had low social status, hence their names were not as exquisite as those of the intelligentsia and scholars. Their methods of naming were based on:

I. Seniority and sequence
E.g. Ruan Xiaoqi阮小七 (Little seven Ruan), Xionger熊二(Second bear), Zhangsan张三(Third Zhang), Lisi李四(Fourth Li).
II. Sum of parents' ages
III. Weight at birth
E.g. Qijin七斤(Seven jin), Liujin六斤(Six jin).

Ancient names of females
In the ancient times, most females had surnames but had no given names. So how could one address them then?
I. Indication of seniority before the surname
Bo伯 or Meng孟 indicates the eldest child, followed by Zhong仲, Shu叔 and Ji季.
E.g. Meng Jiang 孟姜(eldest daughter of the Jiang family), Shu Zhan叔詹(third daughter of the Zhan family).

II. Adding of "ji姬", "niang娘" or "e娥" to the surname

During the Tang Dynasty, females were fond of using "niang娘 (mother/elderly married woman/young woman)", overlapping characters or "zi子". E.g. Hongniang红娘, Yanniang严娘, Jiaoniang娇娘, Baniang八娘, Yingying莺莺, Jiaojiao娇娇, Mianmian绵绵, Shunzi顺子, Xizi喜子, Yanzi颜子.

III. Combining maiden surname and husband's surname

After marriage, a woman would normally merge her own surname with her husband's surname to form a combined surname. E.g. If a Li family daughter had married to the Zhang family, her surname would either become Li or Zhangli.

Women's "maiden name"

In the past, a woman's name was also known as guiming闺名(maiden name), and it was generally kept unknown to others. It would only be used officially when matters of marriage were involved. In traditional marriage, one of the six proprieties observed was "wenming问名(ask name)". Also, after marriage, the maiden name would only be used within the married woman's parents' home but not in her husband's family

6. The Emperor and Names

Name granting and renaming by emperor
Besides granting surnames, the emperor would also grant names and do renaming. The emperor would also give someone a bad name as a form of punishment. E.g. During Tang Dynasty, Wu Zetian changed the names of Qidan chieftains Li Jinzhong and Sun Wanrong to Li Miezhong李灭忠 (Li betrayed loyalty) and Sun Wanzhan孙万斩(Sun beheaded ten thousand times) after they attempted to rebel.

The longest name granted
Qing Dynasty emperor Qianlong once granted his favourite official a very long name that consisted of 12 characters:
e-le-zhe-yi te-mu-er e-er-ke ba-bai
鄂勒哲依忒木尔额尔克巴拜

> He hoped that this subject could enjoy good fortune, longevity, be as strong as the iron and be prized like a treasure.

"e-le-zhe-yi" refers to having good fortune in Mongolian; "te-mu-er" means having longevity; "e-er-ke" means iron and "ba-bai" means treasured one.

Crown Prince or Dog?

7. Imperial Examinations and Names

Scholars in the past studied hard for many years in order to succeed in the imperial examinations.

But few scholars knew that their names would also influence their future prospects in the imperial examinations.

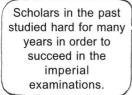

During the Ming Dynasty, Sun Rigong 孙日恭 became the top scorer. But he could not be the Top Scholar because Emperor Yongle did not like his name.

Rigong. Rigong, won't it become the character "Bao 暴 (violent)" when the words are combined?

He found a candidate named Xing Kuan 邢宽.

Xing 邢 and Xing 刑 sound similar. "Xing Kuan" implies good policy.

Therefore, Xing Kuan was selected as the Top Scholar.

During the Qing Dynasty Guangxu era, the top scorer was Zhu Ruzhen 朱汝珍, but the character "zhen" offended Empress Dowager Cixi.

I've just killed Concubine Zhen. Just the sight of the word "zhen" fills me with apprehension.

Cixi lowered Zhu Ruzhen to the second position and chose Liu Chunlin to be the Top Scholar.

May this name "Chunlin 春霖 (spring rain)" bring spring breeze and rain as we're facing a drought now.

Thus Liu Chunlin became the last Top Scholar of China.

8. Childhood Names

Xiaoming小名 refers to childhood name. It is one's unofficial childhood name, usually used by family members and friends as an intimate form of address.

Adopting a humble name
In the past, as sanitation was poor in rural areas and medicine was not easily available, young children were prone to premature death. Parents believed that jianming贱名(humble names) could lengthen one's lifespan, so they liked giving their children humble names or ugly names to avoid the evil and disasters so that they may grow up safely. Such names include Gou Waer狗娃儿(Baby dog),NiuWaer牛娃儿 (Baby cow), Azhu阿猪(Piggy), Agou阿狗 (Doggie).
Tiedan铁蛋(Iron egg), Tiezhu铁柱(Iron pillar) — in hope that the child will be as strong as the iron egg and iron pillar .
Gouzi狗子(Dog) — so that the child can be nurtured as easily as a young dog.
Guokouer锅扣儿 (Wok covered baby) —- do a cupping action upon the child with a wok and he will not die young.

Childhood names of famous people:
Han Gaozu Liu Bang刘邦 – Liu San刘三
Cao Cao曹操   – Aman阿瞒
Liu Chan刘禅   – Adou阿斗
Tai Wudi北魏太武帝   – Feili狒狸
Tao Yuanming陶渊明   – Xigou溪狗
Wang Xianzhi王献之   – Guannu官奴
Lao She老舍   – Xiaogouweiba小狗尾巴
Guo Moruo郭沫若   – Wenbao文豹

9. Interesting Names

In the past history records, there were names which appeared to be feminine but they were actually male names! E.g. Feng Fu冯妇 ("married woman Feng"), Xu Furen徐夫人("Lady Xu"), Ding Furen丁夫人("Lady Ding"), N∣Fang女防(female Fang), Lu N∣sheng鲁女生("schoolgirl Lu"), Yang Poer杨婆儿(woman).

They were not being sissy to have chosen such feminine names. Some of them were even very energetic and strong men!

Feng Fu was not Madam Feng!

| Feng Fu冯妇 was a brave man who was good at hunting tigers. He later changed his work to become a philanthropist. | One day, he met a group of tiger hunters. They failed to catch any tiger, so they invited Feng Fu to hunt for one. | Hence Feng Fu took up his old profession again and killed a tiger. The idiom "zai zuo Feng Fu再作冯妇" is derived from this story. |

Xu Furen was not Lady Xu!

Xu Furen was closely related to the assassination attempt on Emperor Qin Shihuang by Jing Ke!

The dagger which Jing Ke had used to assassinate Emperor Qin was the one which Crown Prince Dan of Yan state had bought from Xu Furen at a high price. It seemed that Xu Furen was no ordinary man!

There were also examples of females having male names. E.g. Sun Quan, the ruler of Wu kingdom during the Three Kingdoms period, had a daughter named Xiaohu 小虎 (Little Tiger); Emperor Xiao Wudi's mother Empress Dowager Lu had a name called Huinan 惠男 ("kind man"); Emperor Han Wudi's wife Lady Wei's original name was Zifu 子夫 ("son of man"); during the Southern Dynasties, Qi imperial maid Han Lanying was called Han Gong 韩公 ("male Han").

Look, in the *Book of Han*, youth Boji 薄姬 ("ji" refers to "woman") and Zhao Zier 赵子儿 ("male child Zhao") were once in courtship.

Boji was a male, while Zhao Zier was a female!

10. Names and Fortune

All sorts of methods have been created to pick a good and auspicious name. If a person's life has not been going well, it is possible to change his luck by changing his name. These methods have no scientific basis, but they reflect everyone's desire for a good life.

The yin yang method
The Chinese people divide all things into yin 阴 and yang 阳. Names, too, have yin and yang elements. When giving a name, it is important to balance yin and yang. If a character has an odd number of strokes, it is yang. If the number of strokes is even, it is yin.

The famous yin yang symbol

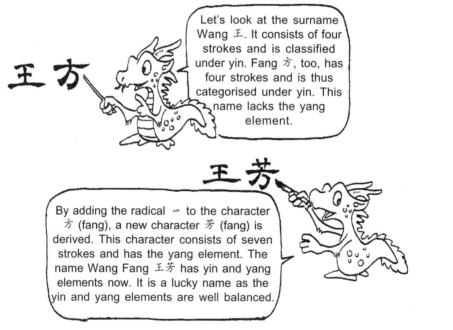

Let's look at the surname Wang 王. It consists of four strokes and is classified under yin. Fang 方, too, has four strokes and is thus categorised under yin. This name lacks the yang element.

By adding the radical ⺿ to the character 方 (fang), a new character 芳 (fang) is derived. This character consists of seven strokes and has the yang element. The name Wang Fang 王芳 has yin and yang elements now. It is a lucky name as the yin and yang elements are well balanced.

Elements method

The ancients believed that all things in the world were made up of the Five Elements. The Five Elements are Metal, Wood, Water, Fire and Earth. These Five Elements support and restrain one another. If the name has supporting qualities, there is balance and good fortune. Conversely, if the name has restraining qualities, it is deemed to be inauspicious.

Diagram of the Five Elements

Restraining
Supporting

Let's call our child 刘森 (Liu Sen).

Wait! That's not an auspicious name.

The radical of the character liu 刘 is jin 金 (Metal). Sen 森 has the radical mu 木 (Wood). In the Five Elements, Metal restrains Wood. No good.

What name is auspicious then?

In the Five Elements, Metal promotes Water. Pick a character with the Water element, for example, hai 海 (sea), yong 泳 (to swim) or jiang 江 (river). That is more auspicious.

Naming based on the Chinese Zodiac

There are 12 signs in the Chinese Zodiac, i.e. 12 animal signs are used to represent the birth years of different individuals: Rat, Ox, Tiger, Rabbit, Dragon, Snake, Horse, Goat, Monkey, Rooster, Dog and Pig. Every individual will have an animal sign that represents the year in which he is born.

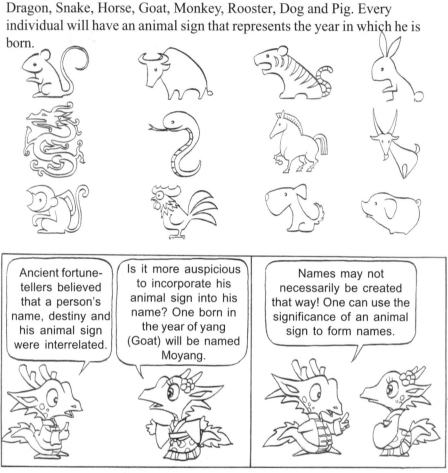

Ancient fortune-tellers believed that a person's name, destiny and his animal sign were interrelated.

Is it more auspicious to incorporate his animal sign into his name? One born in the year of yang (Goat) will be named Moyang.

Names may not necessarily be created that way! One can use the significance of an animal sign to form names.

The Rat, Ox, Rabbit, Horse, Goat, Rooster and Dog are animals which feed on grains. Those who are born under one of these animal signs may want to include characters like "mi米(rice)" or/and "dou豆(bean)" in their names.

The Goat, Horse, Ox and Rabbit are herbivores, those having one of these animal signs may like to include words with a "caozitou草字头(grass as top part of character)" in their names.

11. National and Family Name Taboos

Public or national name taboos
In ancient times, words involving the emperor's name, in spoken or written form, were to be avoided.

Family and private name taboos
One would also avoid the use of his ancestors' and parents' names.

Sage name taboo
Using the names of sages or virtuous people was a taboo, too.

Emperor Mindi of Jin whose name was Sima Ye later changed the city name of Jianye (today's Nanjing) to "Jiankang".

Emperor Wendi of Jin, named Sima Zhao, once changed the name of Wang Zhaojun of the Han Dynasty to Wang Mingjun.

As Tang Gaozu was called Li Yuan, the Tang Dynasty people thus altered the Eastern Jin Dynasty great poet Tao Yuanming's name to Tao Quanming.

By the Song Dynasty, the use of names with similar pronunciations became a taboo as well. As emperor Gaozong was called Zhao Gou, not only was the word "Gou" unusable, more than 50 other words which also had the same pronunciation as "Gou" were avoided.

Even the use of deities' names was a taboo too! Because Han Dynasty Emperor Wendi was named Liu Heng 刘恒, the Chinese mythical goddess of the moon that was originally named "Heng E 姮娥" was renamed as today's "Chang E 嫦娥".

Death penalty for writing the emperor's name!
One could face a fatal disaster if he went against the national taboos. During Qing Dynasty emperor Qianlong's reign, a person by the name of Wang Xihou wrote a book called "Ziguan 字贯" in which the names Xuanhua, Yinzhen and Hongli of emperors Kangxi, Yongzheng and Qianlong respectively were used directly. This infuriated Emperor Qianlong, and thus he ordered everyone in Wang Xihou's family executed.

As for family taboos, as Jin Dynasty great calligrapher Wang Xizhi's father was named Wang Zheng, he wrote "zhengyue正月" (first month of the lunar year) as "chuyue初月" (first moon) instead.

There were also some very exaggerated taboos. During the Song Dynasty, Liu Wensou's father was named Liu Yue. Thus he would not listen to yue乐 (music) all his life, neither would he go to the yue岳 (high mountains).

Xu Ji's father was called Xu Shi, so he would not use any shiqi (stoneware) throughout his life. And whenever he came across stones, he would never step on them. If he needed to cross any stone bridge, he would ask somebody to carry him across.

Talented Poet Vexed over Father's Name

During the Tang Dynasty, Li He was a very talented poet who could compose poems at the age of seven.

With his talent, it should not be a problem for him to be a jinshi进士 (successful candidate in the highest imperial examination), but he would not sit for the examination.

Why didn't you sit for the imperial examination to become a jinshi?

Han Yu

My father's name is Jinsu晋肃. As "Jin晋" and "Jin进" have the same pronunciation, I'll not become a jinshi in order to avoid the name taboo.

Han Yu could not tolerate the absurdity of this kind of taboo and wrote the essay Hui Bian (Debate on Taboos) to refute name taboos.

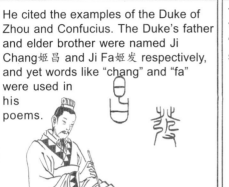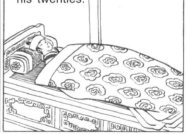

12. Customs of Naming

1. Alias names
Parents used to be worried that their children would die prematurely. So, their children would use a disciple name obtained from the temples but they need not become a monk or nun. The names, gotten under this type of naming custom, were called jiming寄名 (alias names).

The child would pay respect to a Buddhist monk and obtain a religious name. Sometimes, his date of birth would be put in a red pouch called jiming dai which was hung on a Buddhist cabinet.

The monk would give the child some special items such as silver lock and talisman as blessings so that he might avoid illness and disasters, and grow up well without mishap.

When the child grew up, he would give up his alias name before his marriage. He would bring joss sticks and offerings to the temple to redeem his vow, wear a monk's robe and do some sweeping chores.

The monk then used a twig to whip the back of the young man who would in turn remove the monk's robe, drop the broom and run back home, thereby resuming secular life.

The young man would then use his original name instead of his religious name. The jiming dai would be retrieved and taken home.

Lu Xun had an alias name

Eminent writer Lun Xun had an alias name when he was young. Before he turned one, his father took him to Changqing Temple in Shaoxing and he became a disciple of Buddhist monk Longzu. Lu Xun was then bestowed with a Buddhist name "Chang Geng长庚". Fifty-odd years later, Lu Xun wrote "My First Buddhist Monk" to narrate this matter. "Chang Geng" was occasionally used by Lun Xun as his pen name over the years.

2. Calling one's name to summon his spirit

People used to believe that names were more than just a form of address, and were also some form of mystical symbols. One's spirit had connections to his own name.

13. Name Repetition

Similar surnames and names often occur although many characters are available for use in naming.

This has been happening since ancient times. Confucius' disciple Zeng Can was mistaken as a murderer because of this.

Murderer Zengcan

There was once a murderer who had the same name as Zeng Can.

Your son has killed somebody!

Zeng Can's mother was informed.

This is impossible.

Soon, another person came.

My goodness! Your son has killed somebody!

This is impossible.

Then came the third person who told her:

Don't you know that your son has killed somebody?

Looks like my son has really killed somebody!

She climbed over the wall and made haste to escape.

History records of name repetition

The names "Li Guang李广" and "Zhang Heng张衡" of the Han Dynasty were used six times throughout history; "Wang Chong王充", "Zhao Yun赵云" were used four times; During the Han Dynasty, there were two Han Xin韩信 and during the Song Dynasty, nine Zhang Liang张良.

14. Name Riddles

In the classic *Romance of the Three Kingdoms*, Dong Zhuo董卓 was a much detestable character.

But he was powerful and influential. The people were helpless and could do nothing to him. So, they came up with a folk rhyme with his name concealed in it to express their scorn.

It went, "Qianlicao (thousand-li grass), he qingqing (how impressive), shi ri pu (divined to live for ten days), bu de sheng (survive no more)."

Qian千 + li里 = zhong重, and adding the character top part of "cao草" = Dong董
Shi十 + ri日 + pu卜 = Zhuo卓

Here are other name riddles, see if you can work them out.

"Grazing of cows and sheep forbidden." (Guess the name of a Tang Dynasty poet.)

"To evolve new things from the old." (Guess the name of a writer from the modern China era.)

(Continued on the next page)

"Territories of Han Dynasty" (Guess the name of an emperor.)

"Ti 倜"(Guess the name of a writer from the modern China era.)

Answers to the riddles:
1. Du Mu 杜牧 (Du means dujue 杜绝(stop); Mu refers to the herd.)
2. Lao She 老舍 (Lao – old; She – give up)
3. Liu Bang 刘邦(Liu was the surname of Han Dynasty emperors; Bang refers to states.)
4. Zhou Shuren 周树人 (obtained by breaking down the character Ti 倜.)

Part Three:
Courtesy Names and Other Types of Names

In the past, besides surnames and given names, there were also courtesy names. What are courtesy names, and what purpose do they serve? Besides courtesy names, this chapter will cover pseudonyms, nicknames, pen names, professional and other types of names.

1. Courtesy Names

What are courtesy names?
In ancient times, besides having a surname and a given name, one would have a courtesy name "Zi字" as well. The courtesy name was the proper form of address for an adult. On reaching 20 years of age, young men would "put on the hat" as a sign they had reached adulthood. This ritual was held in the ancestral temple, where the boy would bind his hair and put on the ceremonial hat. Then his father or another elder would give him a courtesy name.

> It is now common to say mingzi名字 (literally means given name and courtesy name respectively). But in the past, ming名 and zi字 were used as two separate forms of address.

> Few people these days have courtesy names.

For the ancients, the given name is the essence, the courtesy name represents virtue.
The given name serves to identify, the courtesy name stands for moral integrity.

How courtesy names are assigned

The courtesy name is also known as the style name (or literary name) "Biao Zi表字". The style name and given name were closely linked to each other. Thus the two types of names will definitely have a meaningful relationship.

Synonyms

The given name and courtesy name have the same or similar meanings. E.g. Zhuge Liang诸葛亮(Bright), styled Kongming孔明(Brilliant); Zhou Yu周瑜, styled Gongjin公瑾. (Both Yu and jin mean "beautiful jade" in Chinese.)

Antonyms

The given name and courtesy name are opposite in meaning. E.g. Zhu Xi朱熹(Dawn), styled Yuanhui元晦(Night).

Complementary

The given name and courtesy name together illustrate or create a chain of associations. E.g. Yang Guo杨过, styled Gaizhi改之, has the sense of having undergone correction; Bai Juyi白居易, styled Letian乐天), being optimistic and contented with life, was thus able to stay at ease.

Allusions

The names are drawn from classical works. E.g. Zhao Yun赵云, styled Zilong子龙, comes from "Cloud from Dragon" in the book *I Ching*.

Dividing the name

Breaking apart the parts of the name. E.g. Liu Tong刘侗, styled Tong Ren同人.

Adding a word

Adding another word to the name, e.g. Xie An谢安, styled Anshi安石.

A male member of the nobility would usually have an extra word added before his style name to represent his seniority among his siblings, e.g.Meng孟 or Bo伯 (indicates the eldest child) followed by Zhong仲, Shu叔 and Ji季. Sometimes words like Fu父 or Fu甫 were added after the style names to distinguish gender, e.g. Qu Yuan's father was called Qu Bo Yong Fu屈伯庸父, i.e. Qu was the surname, Bo indicated his seniority, his style name was Yong and Fu was a laudatory title to address a male.

Qu Bo Yong Fu

Cao Meng-de

There are so many different addresses, it makes my head spin!

That's right! When reading the classics, you have to take careful...

...note of names like Bo Qin-fu伯禽父 and Zhong Shan-fu仲山甫. Their surnames are not Bo伯 and Zhong仲!

Appropriate Use of Given Name and Courtesy Name

Given names were used by the family; courtesy names by outsiders. During interpersonal interaction, courtesy names were used instead of given names. When speaking of oneself, using the given name showed humility, while using the courtesy name reflected great arrogance. Addressing others by their courtesy names was considered respectful, whereas usage of their given name was deemed rude. Those of the same standing could address one another by their courtesy names. When teachers and superiors called their students and subordinates by their courtesy names, it showed that the former thought highly of the latter.

Liu Bei刘备, was styled Xuande玄德. Cao Cao addressed him by his courtesy name. When Liu Bei referred to himself, he used his given name.

Did women have courtesy names as well?

Only the nobility and higher-class women had courtesy names. Most women had only one name, also known as the maiden name, throughout their lives, though a few famous women had their courtesy names on historical record:
Wang Qiang, styled Zhaojun,
Ban Zhao, styled Huiban and
Cai Yan, styled Wenji.

2. Pseudonyms and Nicknames

Pseudonyms
A pseudonym (bie hao 别号) was another way to address oneself in addition to the given name and courtesy name. One would get to choose his favourite pseudonym, and he might have many pseudonyms in his lifetime.

Pseudonym based on the place of residence
Tao Yuanming 陶渊明, pseudonym Mr Wuliu 五柳先生 (there were five willows growing by his house).

Pseudonym based on personal interests or feelings
Lu You 陆游, pseudonym Fangweng 放翁 (signifying his lack of regard for status, influence or etiquette).

Phrases like xiansheng 先生 (Mr), laoren 老人 (OldMan), weng 翁 (Father), jushi 居士 (Lay Buddhist), daoren 道人 (Taoist) and shanren 山人 (Mountain Man) were popular elements in pseudonyms. E.g. Qinglian Jushi 青莲居士 (Tang poet Li Bai), Shaoling Yelao 少陵野老 (Tang poet Du Fu) and Shangu Daoren 山谷道人 (Northern Song Dynasty calligrapher Huang Tingjian).

Nicknames

Nicknames are generally given and widely acknowledged by others. They are often humorous, mocking and sarcastic. Nicknames are casually used, largely based on appearances, personalities, abilities and so on.

Some nicknames of characters from *Water Margin*

"The Resourceful Wizard" Wu Yong "智多星"吴用

"Black Whirlwind" Li Kui "黑旋风"李逵

"Flowery Monk" Lu Zhishen. "花和尚"鲁智深

"Panther Head" Lin Chong "豹子头"林冲

"Blue-Faced Beast" Yang Zhi "青面兽"杨志

"Female Yaksha" Sun Erniang "母夜叉"孙二娘

Nicknames also reflect the sentiments of the people.

The famous Song Dynasty magistrate Bao Zheng, who was uncompromising, unmoved by status and influence, impartial and incorruptible, was much loved by the people. Thus he was nicknamed as Bao Qingtian包青天 (Blue Sky Bao).

Yu Chenglong of the Qing Dynasty led a simple and frugal life, living on plain food and rice and eating only green vegetables although he held a high ranking post in the Ministry of War. Hence he ended up with the nickname Yu Qingcai于青菜 (Green Vegetables Yu).

The earliest nickname
Nicknames were first adopted during the Xia Dynasty with despot Jie being possibly the first in history to receive a nickname. He was called "Moves Large Beast移大牺" because he was very strong and able to push an ox over.

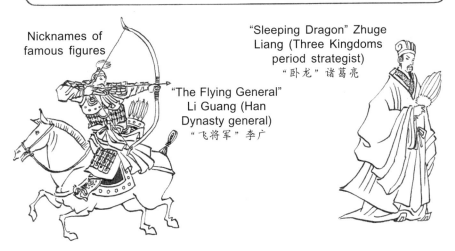

Nicknames of famous figures

"The Flying General" Li Guang (Han Dynasty general)
"飞将军"李广

"Sleeping Dragon" Zhuge Liang (Three Kingdoms period strategist)
"卧龙"诸葛亮

The Roar of the Lioness of Hedong

Song Dynasty poet Su Shi had a friend named Chen Jichang whose wife was very fierce. Visitors to his home often witnessed Jichang being scolded very loudly by his wife Liu.

Useless man! Hand over this month's money for the daily necessities!

Su Shi later composed a poem teasing Chen Jichang:
"Poor Resident of Dragon Hill! Idly speaking of staying up all night. Once he hears the sudden roar of the lioness of Hedong, he drops his cane, and his heart is seized with fear."

"Lioness of Hedong" later became Liu's nickname, and "The Roar of the Hedong Lioness" came to be used as a description of the angry rebuke of a fierce woman.

3. Pen Names and Stage Names

Pen names

Have you read the works of Li Yaotang, Wan Jiabao, Shu Qingchun and Xie Wanying before?

Who are they?

Li Shaotang, Wan Jiabao, Shu Qingchun and Xie Wanying are actually famous modern Chinese writers.
Li Yaotang 李尧棠 – Ba Jin 巴金,
Wan Jiabao 万家宝 – Cao Yu 曹禺,
Shu Qingchun 舒庆春 – Lao She 老舍,
Xie Wanying 谢婉莹 – Bing Xin 冰心.

Ba Jin, Cao Yu, Lao She and Bing Xin are all pen names (bi ming 笔名) known around the world. These writers gained their reputations under their *noms de plume*, such that few know them by their original names. An author can use many pen names: Lu Xun 鲁迅 once used more than 140 pen names.

Besides concealing the author's identity, pen names can also be used to express the writer's personality and aspiration.

Reasons to use a pen name
Lu Xun
Originally named Zhou Shuren. He published *The Diary of a Madman* under this pen name in 1918. His pen name is significant in three ways – expressing his love for his mother Lu Rui; an encouragement for the foolish ones (Lu means foolish) to stop procrastinating and quickly get things done (Xun means fast); and finally, Zhou and Lu were historically of the same family.

Bing Xin
Bing Xin's pen name is derived from a verse by Tang Dynasty poet Wang Changling – "If my kin and friends in Luoyang ask after me, say "a sheet of ice-heart in a jade vase". By choosing the name Bing Xin (ice-heart), she expresses her purity of heart, open nature and untainted character.

Qiong Yao
The famous Taiwanese writer's original name is Chen Zhe. Her pen name Qiong Yao comes from the poem "Papaya" in *The Book of Songs*: "I was given a peach, and I repaid him with a beautiful jade (Qiong Yao) in return."

Stage names

Stage names (yi ming艺名) are used by artistes when they make their debut. Many artistes adopt unique and striking stage names to attract the audience's attention, e.g. Monkey Xiaoyang小杨猴, Red Peony牡丹红, Flying Over Grasses草上飞, Popular Every Month月月红, New Phoenix Cloud新凤霞, One Flag Pole一杆旗, etc. Stage names may be used to reflect one's hopes, strengths or even indicate a mentor. Take, for instance, the well-known Peking Opera actor Yang Yuelou杨月楼. His son succeeded his aspiration and adopted the stage name "Yang Xiaolou杨小楼" (Little Lou).

China has the earliest record of artistes using stage names. The first artiste on record using a stage name might be Zhao Feiyan. She was originally named Zhao Yizhu and was a dancer in the household of Princess Pingyang when Emperor Chengdi took her into the imperial palace and made her his empress. Because she could dance beautifully, seemingly as light as a swallow, he bestowed the name of Feiyan (Flying Swallow) on her.

4. Era Names and Posthumous Names

Era Names

Era names (nian hao年号) are reign titles adopted by an emperor on ascending the throne, counting years from the start of his reign. They are considered to have begun with Emperor Han Wudi, who declared the new era Jianyuan on coming to power. During the Ming and Qing Dynasties, most emperors preferred to stay with one era name, though Emperor Han Wudi went through 11 during his reign. Sometimes the era name may also be used to refer to the emperor, such as Emperors Kangxi and Qianlong.

Posthumous names

After the death of an emperor or high official, the imperial court would assign a laudatory or critical posthumous name (shi hao谥号) based on his deeds and character when he was alive. Positive posthumous names would be words like wen文 (civil) and wu武 (martial), while negative ones would be words like li厉 (severe) and you幽 (darkened).

Part Four: The Chinese Way of Addressing

To the Chinese, the way of addressing oneself and others is as important as their etiquette. Different names are used to address oneself and others. In this chapter, we shall introduce the modest and respectful forms of address, as well as the Chinese way of addressing people through the ages.

2. Self-referential and Referential

Self-referential

Bi Ren鄙人(I/Your humble servant): Bi originally referred to somebody who lived in the city outskirts. In the olden days, most people of a high status would reside within the city walls, while those who lived outside the city walls were considered to be country bumpkins.

Untalented不才: Referred to somebody with no special abilities or talent.

Unworthy不肖: Referred to somebody who lacked virtue, thus would be unable to perpetuate his ancestors' great achievement and moral integrity.

Chen臣(Subject), Qie妾(Concubine): In olden times, a man would become somebody's subject, a woman would become somebody's concubine. A man would therefore call himself a subject/servant, while a woman would call herself a concubine.

Pupil晚生, Young Scholar后学, Shallow Scholar末学: "Shallow Scholar" was used to imply one's shallow knowledge. This was how a junior would call himself when speaking to a senior.

Common People小人: Self-reference of a minister to his king, also used by the common people to address themselves in a humble way

Zhen朕 (Sovereign): Used by a sovereign in addressing himself. Before the era of the first Emperor Qin Shihuang, the name could be used by a royal person in proclamations instead of "I". During his reign, "Zheng" was used exclusively by him. He humbly addressed himself as "Gua Ren寡人" which is derived from "Gua De Zhi Ren寡德之人(One who has few virtues.)".

Referential Forms of Address to Others:

Zi 子: An olden form of addressing a learned scholar, for e.g., Kongzi (Confucius), Laozi, Mengzi (Mencius), Mozi and Zhuangzi.

Master夫子: A respectful way of addressing an elder.

Mister/Sir/Teacher先生: Title of respect to a learned person, teacher or man.

Gong公(Duke or Honourable), Jun君(Gentleman): "Gong" was used to address a person with fame and position, "Jun" was used to address one's peers and juniors.

Ge Xia阁下: Used to address someone in an important official position. In today's modern society, "Ge Xia" is still used in some formal situations.

How is your father getting on?

Thanks for your concern. Ling Zun令尊 is fine.¹

This is Ling Zi令子 Xiao Ming.²

Xiao Ming, greet uncle.

It is common that we use self-referential and deferential names during our social interaction with people. But be careful not to confuse one thing with another.

In the above two situations illustrated, the self-referential and deferential names have all been used wrongly.

People of the olden times were used to adding an extra word "Zun尊 (Honourable)" when addressing an elder or senior. If one was of a lower position, then the word "Xian 贤(Virtuous)" would be used instead. For example, Zun Fumu尊父母(Honourable parents), Xian Di贤弟(Virtuous brother), Xian Qi贤妻(Virtuous wife), Xian Zhi贤侄(Virtuous nephew). Nowadays, "Ling Zun令尊 (Your father)", "Ling Lang令郎(Your son)" and "Ling Ai令爱(Your daughter)" are also often used to address somebody's relatives.

1: correct reply: Thanks for your concern. Jia Fu家父 is fine.
2: correct introduction: This is Xiao'er小儿 Xiao Ming.

In some families, couples do not usually address each other by their names. Instead, the wife will call her husband "Family Head 当家的", "The Outside One 外头的"; The husband will call his wife "Family Head Mistress 内当家的", "Cook 做饭的", "The Inside One 屋里的".

Outsiders will address the married man or woman as "So-and-so's husband", "So-and-so's wife". For couples who have children, others will address the child's father and mother as "So-and-so's father" and "So-and-so's mother" respectively.

3. Forms of Address from Ancient to Modern Times

Miss小姐: During the Song Dynasty, the title of "Miss" was used to address young ladies (for example, imperial maidservant, personal attendant concubine, artisan, prostitute) of a low and degrading status. During the Yuan and Ming Dynasties, the daughters of officials and well-to-do families were called "Miss". "Miss" was later used, even until today, to address any young lady.

Niang娘(Mother): Very often, we come across a child addressing his mother as "Niang" in ancient dramas or novels. In the past, "Niang" was actually also used to address a young lady, and it was later used generally to address a woman.

Ge/Ge Ge哥/哥哥(Brother): "Ge Ge"is a respectful form of address for an elder brother. During the Tang Dynasty, some would address their fathers as "Ge". In the *Old Tang History,* Yuanzong元宗 (Xuanzong玄宗) mentioned, "Fourth Ge四哥is benevolent and filial…" The "Fourth Ge" in this context refers to his father Ruizong睿宗(Ruizong was the fourth in order). In fact, a father would even address himself as "Ge Ge" when speaking to his son. In a letter which Tang Taizong唐太宗 wrote to his son Tang Gaozong唐高宗, he addressed himself as "Ge Ge Chi哥哥敕".

Jie/Jie Jie姐/姐姐(Sister): In ancient times, "Jie Jie" was used when one addressed his mother, or used when a father called his daughter. In addition, prostitutes were called "Jie Jie".

Relationship Chart: Maternal

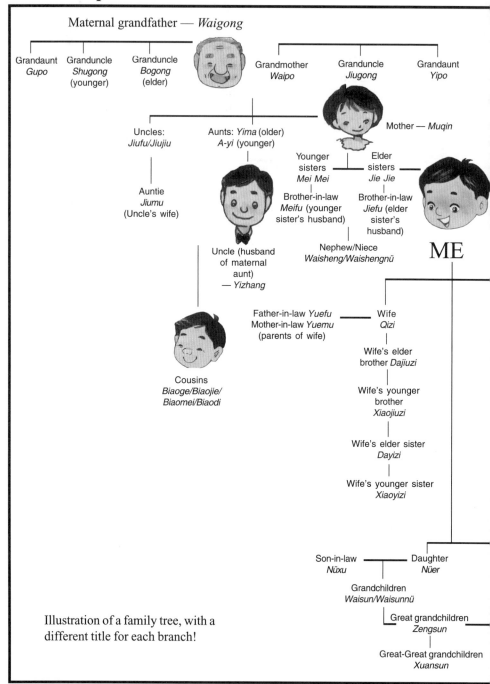

Illustration of a family tree, with a different title for each branch!

Relationship Chart: Paternal

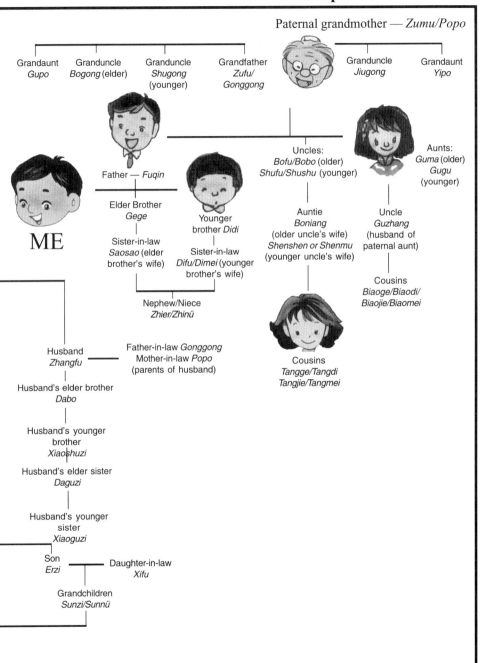

Index of Chinese Family Names

		Page No.			Page No.
白	Bai	70	贺	He	79
蔡	Cai	92	洪	Hong	74
曹	Cao	66	侯	Hou	75
常	Chang	70	胡	Hu	54
陈	Chen	43	黄	Huang	45
程	Cheng	70	贾	Jia	76
崔	Cui	78	江	Jiang	76
戴	Dai	91	姜	Jiang	77
邓	Deng	68	蒋	Jiang	93
丁	Ding	78	金	Jin	76
董	Dong	71	康	Kang	93
杜	Du	72	孔	Kong	80
段	Duan	72	赖	Lai	94
范	Fan	72	雷	Lei	73
方	Fang	73	李	Li	38
冯	Feng	92	梁	Liang	59
傅	Fu	73	廖	Liao	82
高	Gao	58	林	Lin	56
龚	Gong	74	刘	Liu	42
顾	Gu	75	龙	Long	82
郭	Guo	55	卢	Lu	78
韩	Han	65	陆	Lu	82
郝	Hao	75	吕	Lü	77
何	He	57	罗	Luo	61

		Page No.			Page No.
马	Ma	53	吴	Wu	49
毛	Mao	94	武	Wu	87
孟	Meng	81	夏	Xia	87
牛	Niu	82	萧	Xiao	69
潘	Pan	93	谢	Xie	63
彭	Peng	83	熊	Xiong	87
钱	Qian	83	徐	Xu	50
秦	Qin	84	许	Xu	67
邱	Qiu	79	薛	Xue	84
任	Ren	84	严	Yan	88
邵	Shao	85	阎	Yan	88
沈	Shen	94	杨	Yang	44
施	Shi	85	姚	Yao	88
石	Shi	85	叶	Ye	89
史	Shi	85	尹	Yin	90
宋	Song	62	于	Yu	95
苏	Su	86	余	Yu	90
孙	Sun	51	袁	Yuan	89
谭	Tan	86	曾	Zeng	90
唐	Tang	64	张	Zhang	41
田	Tian	89	赵	Zhao	46
万	Wan	94	郑	Zheng	60
汪	Wang	86	钟	Zhong	91
王	Wang	40	周	Zhou	48
韦	Wei	86	朱	Zhu	52
魏	Wei	95	邹	Zou	91

A Brief Chronology of Chinese History

夏 Xia Dynasty			About 2100 – 1600 BC
商 Shang Dynasty			About 1600 – 1100 BC
周 Zhou Dynasty	西周 Western Zhou Dynasty		About 1100 – 771 BC
	東周 Eastern Zhou Dynasty		770 – 256 BC
	春秋 Spring and Autumn Period		770 – 476 BC
	戰國 Warring States		475 – 221 BC
秦 Qin Dynasty			221 – 207 BC
漢 Han Dynasty	西漢 Western Han		206 BC – AD 24
	東漢 Eastern Han		25 – 220
三國 Three Kingdoms	魏 Wei		220 – 265
	蜀漢 Shu Han		221 – 263
	吳 Wu		222 – 280
西晉 Western Jin Dynasty			265 – 316
東晉 Eastern Jin Dynasty			317 – 420
南北朝 Northern and Southern Dynasties	南朝 Southern Dynasties	宋 Song	420 – 479
		齊 Qi	479 – 502
		梁 Liang	502 – 557
		陳 Chen	557 – 589
	北朝 Northern Dynasties	北魏 Northern Wei	386 – 534
		東魏 Eastern Wei	534 – 550
		北齊 Northern Qi	550 – 577
		西魏 Western Wei	535 – 556
		北周 Northern Zhou	557 – 581
隋 Sui Dynasty			581 – 618
唐 Tang Dynasty			618 – 907
五代 Five Dynasties	後梁 Later Liang		907 – 923
	後唐 Later Tang		923 – 936
	後晉 Later Jin		936 – 946
	後漢 Later Han		947 – 950
	後周 Later Zhou		951 – 960
宋 Song Dynasty	北宋 Northern Song Dynasty		960 – 1127
	南宋 Southern Song Dynasty		1127 – 1279
遼 Liao Dynasty			916 – 1125
金 Jin Dynasty			1115 – 1234
元 Yuan Dynasty			1271 – 1368
明 Ming Dynasty			1368 – 1644
清 Qing Dynasty			1644 – 1911
中華民國 Republic of China			1912 – 1949
中華人民共和國 People's Republic of China			1949 –

HISTORY

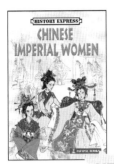

Chinese Imperial Women
The harem was a place where only the most beautiful, intelligent, fortunate and ruthless women could rise to the top. This book tells the stories of these women, the outstanding, the outrageous, the glorious and the tragic ones of the Chinese imperial harem.
160pp, ISBN 978-981-229-482-1

NEW

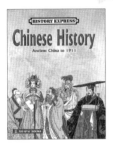

Chinese History: Ancient China to 1911
This book will help you to comprehend and interpret China's history in its proper context, plus provide vivid illustrations, and questions and answers to enhance your appreciation of great people and happenings.
192pp, ISBN 981-229-439-2

Great Chinese Emperors: Tales of Wise and Benevolent Rule
Read the tales of wise and benevolent rulers including Shennong, Li Shimin (Tang dynasty) and Emperor Kangxi (Qing dynasty). These stand tall for their outstanding contributions and character.
192pp, ISBN 981-229-451-1

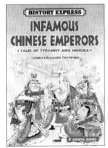

Infamous Chinese Emperors: Tales of Tyranny and Misrule
Stories of China's most notorious emperors who are a motley crew of squanderers, murderers, thugs and lechers, and how they got their just deserts!
192pp, ISBN 981-229-459-7

STRATEGY & LEADERSHIP SERIES

These English comics will heighten your understanding and observations of life for good decision-making and human relationships. Educational and entertaining for the whole family.

The Art of Command: Wei Liao Zi's Strategies of War
Wei Liao was an astute political observer and brilliant strategist with a superb grasp of civil and military measures critical to a state's survival. His work has been hailed as a distinguished work of military science with principles on par with Sun Zi's.

The Art of Tactics: Winning Strategies of Wu Zi
Wu Zi, who was praised by famed Legalist Li Li for surpassing Sima Rangju and Sun Zi, was superb at translating strategies into action. Here, he delves into topics like resolving tactical situations, evaluating the enemy, responding to change, and stimulating one's followers.

The Art of Winning: Wisdom of Tang Tai Zong and Duke Li of Wei
In question-and-answer format, this war-wise emperor and his intrepid commander take us through the logic of winning battles, analysing examples drawn from their own experience and from history's famous battles.

Strategies from the Three Kingdoms
The war stratagems and military teachings which emerged from the Three Kingdoms Period have influenced the way later generations view leadership and power. These strategies are still universally relevant in today's corporate culture as well as warfare.

Sima's Rules of War: The Practice of Dynamic Leadership
Famed War Minister Tian Rangju shares his experience in planning for campaigns, handling warfare, strategising for victory and much more!

Supreme Wisdom: The Art of Insight
Supreme Wisdom is part one of the classic *Gems of Chinese Wisdom*. The characters in the 32 stories here will impress you with their insight and ingenuity!

Sunzi's Art of War: World's Most Famous Military Classic
This famous military classic covers the full spectrum of strategising. Containing extensive knowledge, dealt with in great depth, it is a crystallisation of human wisdom.

Sun Bin's Art of War: World's Greatest Military Treatise
The household Chinese name Sunzi refers to the great military strategist Sun Wu, as well as his descendant Sun Bin, who was framed and crippled but went on to win countless wars and to write the brilliant *Art of War*. Be inspired by his tenacity and wisdom.

Chinese Business Strategies
Offering 30 real-life, ancient case studies with comments on their application in today's business world, this book contains tips useful to the aspiring entrepreneur.

Golden Rules: Tao Zhugong's Art of Business
A collection of Tao Zhugong's principles for business success, this inspiring and penetrating book contains 12 Golden Standards and 12 Golden Safeguards.

100 Strategies of War: Brilliant Tactics in Action
This book captures the essence of extensive military knowledge and practice, and explores the use of psychology in warfare, the importance of diplomatic ties with the enemy's neighbours, the use of reconnaissance and espionage, etc.

Gems of Chinese Wisdom: Mastering the Art of Leadership
Wise up with this delightful collection of tales and anecdotes on the wisdom of great men and women in Chinese history like Confucius, Meng Changjun and Gou Jian.

Thirty-six Stratagems: Secret Art of War
A Chinese military classic that emphasises deceptive schemes to achieve military objectives, this book has caught the attention of military authorities and general readers alike.

Sixteen Strategies of Zhuge Liang: The Art of Management
With advice on how a king should govern the country, establish harmonious relations with his subjects and use reward and punishment to win his people's trust, this is a boon for those involved in business management.

Three Strategies of Huang Shi Gong: The Art of Government
Reputedly one of man's oldest monograph on military strategy, it unmasks the secrets behind brilliant military manoeuvres, clever deployment and control of subordinates, as well as effective government.

Six Strategies for War: The Practice of Effective Leadership
A powerful book for administrators and leaders, it covers critical areas in management and warfare. These include how to recruit talents, manage the state, beat the enemy, lead wisely and manoeuvre brilliantly.

Thirty-six Business Stratagems: Secret Art of War for Today's Entrepreneurs
You can learn through some 100 case studies how entrepreneurs and business people apply the **36 Stratagems** to win over customers and stay agile in a fast-changing business environment.

Total Victory: Sunzi's Art of Business
By using a simple and humorous art form, Wang Xuanming has made the military principles practical for all business and corporate players using 100 case studies.

PHILOSOPHY

ZEN INSPIRATION
Zen is a way of creative living. In this book, you will find out about Zen in all its vitality and simplicity. Whatever it is about Zen that fascinates you – silent meditation or creative expression – you will not be disappointed as you dip into the pages of this book.
Illustrated by **Fu Chunjiang**. *224pp, 150x210mm, ISBN 981-229-455-4.*

INSPIRATION FROM CONFUCIUS:
Choice Quotations from the Analects
More than 100 choice quotations classified under broad themes depicting Confucian core values and enhanced by inspirational thoughts. With additional features on Confucius' life, achievements and influence, it makes an excellent representation of the *Analects*.
Illustrated by **Jeffrey Seow**. *224pp, 150x210mm, ISBN 981-229-398-1.*

THE TAO INSPIRATION :
Essence of Lao Zi's Wisdom
Written more than 2,500 years ago, the Tao Te Ching now comes in 21st century style. Presenting Lao Zi's masterpiece in a concise, comprehensive yet profound manner, this book provides practical wisdom for leadership and for achieving balance and harmony in everyday life.
Illustrated by **Feng Ge**. *176pp, 150x210mm, ISBN 981-229-396-5.*

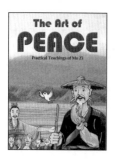

THE ART OF PEACE
The perfect companion if daily stories on war and terrorism are tiring you out. Learn how Mo Zi spread his message of peace to warring states locked in endless conflicts and power struggles.
Illustrated by **Chan Kok Sing**, *152pp, 150x210mm, ISBN 981-229-390-6.*

HEALTHY LIFE

Essential Chinese Medicine Series

A major new series on Chinese herbs, their characteristics, how to tell genuine from fake, their preparations, and how to use Chinese herbs in everyday food dishes to boost your vitality and health. Suitable for laymen and practitioners.

*192x255mm, 240pp, **full colour.***
Health Tonics *ISBN 978-981-229-468-5,*
Restoring Balance *ISBN 978-981-229-469-2,*
Improving Blood Circulation *ISBN 978-981-229-470-8,*
Relieving Wind *ISBN 978-981-229-471-5,*
Treating Common Ailments *ISBN 978-981-229-472-2,*
Healthy Digestion *ISBN 978-981-229-473-9*

* Written and compiled by accredited academics and physicians
* Text in both English and Chinese
* Photographs in full colour

Visit us at
www.asiapacbooks.com
for more information on Asiapac titles.

You will find:
- ▲ Asiapac - The Company
- ▲ Asiapac Logo
- ▲ Asiapac Publications

| Culture | Classics | Jokes & Humour |

- ▲ Comics Extracts
- ▲ Book Reviews
- ▲ New Publications
- ▲ Ordering Our Publications

| History | Philosophy | Healthy Life | Language |

To order books or write to us:
asiapacbooks@pacific.net.sg

中华姓名的故事

编著：亚太编辑部

绘画：傅春江

翻译：庄茹霖、蔡玮宁

 亚太图书有限公司出版